POWER GREATER THAN OURSELVES

i

Other books by Earl Jabay:

The Kingdom of Self
The God-Players
Precisely How to Take Care of Your Self

POWER GREATER THAN OURSELVES

EARL JABAY

Author of

The God Players, The Kingdom of Self

and

Precisely How to Take Care of Your Self

Contents

1

The Birth of Power

Picture a newborn baby, just a few weeks old. If we could have a conversation with the child, perhaps it would go something like this:

"Child, you have just gone through a most difficult and dangerous event—human birth. Were you afraid?"

"No, not at all. You see, I have no knowledge of what could have gone wrong. I am here, and I know of no other place to be."

"Do you need anything?"

"No. I *have* everything. I am fed, burped and my diaper is dry. And I am warm. I am sure there is nothing in the whole world that I need. I think that the world is a nice place."

"But we are worried about the world into which you have been born. It is in sad shape. Humanity seems to learn nothing from its past mistakes. We are losing ground."

"Oh, I don't agree at all. People can have anything they wish to have. There are no limits to what we can possess. I know this because my parents have placed no restraints at all on what I want. They give me anything I want."

"Having now spent a few weeks among us, is there anything you would like to say?"

"Yes. My mind is filling with endless possibilities. There is nothing I cannot do or have. My parents have set no limitations upon me.

"Moreover, I have power. When I cry, mother or father holds me. When I am wet, I cry and they change my diaper. I cannot recall once that they have not done what I needed to have done. It appears to me

1

that I have total power over father and mother and, through them, over my whole environment!"

What is the point of this little dialogue? I am trying to show that a baby comes into the world as his own highest power. He does what he wishes. No one tells him what to do. From the moment he arrives in the world, he makes demands, and his parents make very sure they meet each of those demands. Father works hard to pay the household bills. Mother tends to his daily and hourly needs. Together they feed, clothe and shelter him.

How does this month-old baby get such power over his parents? Simply by his presence. All he needs to do is utter a cry. The cry gives him power over his parents. The baby, therefore, comes into his family as the highest power in his world.

Put a little differently, we can say that the young child is totally absorbed in himself and his own needs. It *must* be that way. God has a very good reason for making babies totally self-concerned: it is the way in which they survive. Babies would never make it into adulthood if they were not, at the beginning of life, totally pre-occupied with themselves and the use of their superior power over others.

Here is a diagram of what we are taking about.

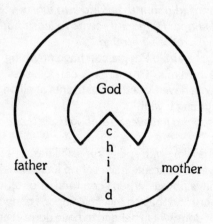

The Birth of Power

Let the outer circle represent the world into which the baby is born. Parents, assuming that they have surrendered to God as the Highest Power in their lives, are ranged on the limits of the circle. God's place is in the center of the world, the place of highest power and authority. Place is also given to the newborn child in the center of the world where he shares with God the position of highest power.

The diagram allows us to see the problem that the child will encounter as he grows older. Sometime, somewhere, somehow, this human being must leave his Father-God's house and recognize Him as the *sole* highest power in the universe. Unless that critical time of second birth is reached, the person whose life began with such glorious power, will be doomed to live out his days in the constant, unending delusion that he is his own highest power. The whole purpose of his life will then have been wasted! When his time comes to die, he will have lived to no purpose. As he came into life, so will he leave. This is the worst of all possible tragedies!

It is usually mother who first challenges the infant's claim to be the highest power in his world. She does this the first time she lets the baby cry without responding to him. A good mother does this after she has fed the baby, burped him, changed his diaper and made him comfortable. When a child cries after all of his needs have been met, it only means that he wants attention.

When a child's mother first sends him the message that he is not going to get all he wants, it is one of the most crucial moments in his life.

That message *must* be sent. The child has no other way of knowing that he is not king of the world. We all know mothers and fathers, however, who seldom send such messages to their demanding infants. There are parents who never let their babies cry because it makes them feel they are not doing their job. If they do not respond immediately to their child, regardless of the circumstances, they feel guilty. They quickly pick up the crying child and comfort him. By doing this, they send him a clear message that he possesses greater power than they.

It is a battle of wills, parents' against the child's. In such a battle, it is terribly important for the child to lose.

If he loses, there is good prospect that he will become a solid human being, that is, a being, secondary to God.

If he keeps on winning and the parents keep losing, the child is doomed to live out his life playing god, harming his relationships with others and imperiling himself. His parents, purely out of their need for self-survival, will either recede from the life of their child for their own protection, or be crushed by him. The child has only one path open to him—relentless self-destruction—and in the end, but for the grace of God, an earned suffering.

I must at this point deal with the objections of those who are horrified by the harshness of my suggestions. "Is there no place," it might be asked, "for tender, loving care? Does not a child need to be loved, appreciated and affirmed from the very beginning of his life? And is it not a fact that the bonding between the child and his parents must take place in these early weeks of life, if the child is to develop normally?"

To these good questions, I want to answer affirmatively and with full conviction. When it comes to the need for love, affirmation and understanding in dealing with our children, you will hear my voice raised above all others. There is no doubt that all parents today need help in learning how to really love their children.

I would want to add, however, that discipline—some people call it tough love—is one of the highest forms of love. It is not enough to say yes to the bumper-sticker question "Have you hugged your kid today?" Someone should print another sticker asking, "Have you disciplined your kid today?" If you do not correct him, how will your kid understand that you love him? Loving discipline is one of the highest forms of love.

When does one begin this loving discipline? When the child is two years old? Two *months* old? No. Parents should begin in the first week of the infant's life. Why so early? Because that is when the power begins. Even by that time the child is using his un-defined, uncircumscribed power on his parents and using it effectively.

The Birth of Power

Now we are able to see clearly that each person is born with the gift of a complete package of power. The package, in a certain sense, is without limits because no one has stepped forward to define the limits. Parents are supposed to do this. Unfortunately, they never do the job adequately. In some cases, they hardly do it at all. The result is a spoiled child, and later, a troubled adult. Such a child remains his own highest power. From a theological viewpoint, he is in the position of God.

It is crucial that the parents of a very young infant understand that they are dealing with an ego that is infinite in size. If the parents can really understand and accept that fact, then they are, from the very first, in a position to lovingly discipline the child.

On the other hand, if the parents see their darling infant as quite powerless and allow him to win in the contest of wills, they will see nothing wrong in pampering and spoiling him. Parents who view the ego-power of their child as weak, undeveloped and innocent, are doomed to a terrible fate: they will live out their lives with god-playing children who never become adults.

All this, of course, is in conflict with the current secular psychological and psychiatric understandings.

Almost all modern psychologies see the child as basically (1) powerless and (2) victimized by bad authorities. To talk about a newborn having an innate tendency toward evil seems like utter nonsense to them. "Who in his right mind today," they ask, "takes seriously the theological doctrine of original sin?"

Many of us! More, I hope, than secular psychologists would think. And there are all kinds of clinical evidence that the doctrine is true. It is not only true. It works!

Christian parents have known for centuries that you must break the will of the child. Susannah Wesley, who had nineteen children, said that the will of a child—but not his spirit—had to be broken by the time he was two years old. And look at the results, particularly John and Charles!

Many Christian parents today are succeeding marvelously with the task of parenting simply by insisting upon obedience in their children. These parents have a Christian philosophy of life which they are putting into practice with their children. They do not hesitate to say that their children are sinners and that it is necessary to stand lovingly against the will of a child from the very beginning of his life.

We have talked about the birth of power. Now, I want to say something here about the death of power.

Power in a human being ends when, finally, after a long, painful struggle, a person finally surrenders to a Power greater than himself.

Good parenting, which consistently teaches the practice of obedience to authority, will greatly help the child in taking that critical step of learning to obediently submit to God. Yet, even where obedience to authority has been well taught, the act of surrender to God kills us, and keeps on stabbing us as we continue to painfully die to self in order to live to God.

In the case where children are poorly parented, their pain in living as adults is enormous, though it can be somewhat mitigated by wealth, a healthy body, a clever mind and good friends. Auto-salvation from the tyranny of oneself, however, is nothing but a false victory. Better to die to self and get it over with. Poorly parented people usually come to that initial point of surrender to God (which always registers as death) only after they have lost everything and been stripped of the persons and things they hold dear. It is the point at which one comes to the end of himself. He has no answers, no plans, no more excuses. He is at the bottom of the bottom of the world.

Even in that deep, dark hell, a person may choose not to surrender. He may choose to keep bouncing at the bottom of his world. It can be a fatal, tragic, final choice.

My friends in Alcoholics Anonymous know what I am talking about here because they are my teachers. Those of us who are not in AA are really no different from our alcoholic friends. I am convinced that all of us begin life by making Self central. The solution of our common problem is the same—a loving God who rescues us from ourselves. But for the grace of God, none of us would ever stop perishing on the bottom of the world. But for the grace of God, none of us would begin to live again. Nobody can explain this. Nobody should try. We simply know that once our power is dead, the perfect Power who is God can make the dead live again.

Long ago, God showed the prophet Ezekiel a vision in which a valley was filled with dry, human bones.

"Son of man, can these bones live?" asked the Lord.

Ezekiel was not too sure. Then God commanded the prophet to say, "O dry bones, hear the word of the Lord. Thus says the Lord God to these bones: Behold, I will cause breath to enter you, and you shall live."

And that is what happened in the vision: "there was a noise, and behold, a rattling; and the bones came together, bone to its bone" (Ezekiel 37:1-7).

It was a demonstration that when all power in us finally dies, the God of all power begins His re-creative work.

2

Power in Young Children

In the course of family life, parents often find power burdensome and cast it away. Invariably, if they do this, it is quickly snatched up and pocketed by their children. The power of young children over their parents is awesome and impressive. It is also a sad and tragic thing to see. A few examples will show what I mean.

A mother with her four-year-old daughter are shopping in the supermarket. The grocery cart is almost filled and mother is relieved that this tedious task is nearly over with. She already has an eye on a cashier with a miraculously short line.

Unfortunately the last aisle she passes contains the candy display. And here a problem develops.

"I want that candy bar," announces mother's little helper. Her hot little hands reach out and grab it from the shelf.

"Put it back. I'm in a hurry," says mother.

"I *want* it. C'mon. Why can't I have it?"

"Because I'm in a hurry. Besides, we just had lunch."

Her daughter persists. "But I helped you with the shopping!"

"Yes, you were a good helper but— Look, others are getting ahead of us in the line."

The four-year-old senses it is time for the confrontation. "I want this candy bar, and if I don't get it, I'm going to scream!" Her voice is shrill and the candy bar already in hand. "I *want* it!"

Mother, having no heart for a public showdown, weakens. "Oh, all right. Just this once, if you *promise* to be a good girl!"

POWER GREATER THAN OURSELVES

"I promise," says the little queen to her powerless mother.

Here is another example. True story.

I am counseling the parents of three children aged twelve, seven and five. The parents reached out to me because the oldest was not doing well in school and the youngest was becoming a disciplinary problem. In the course of our conversation, I asked how many hours of TV the children were watching each day. It took a little coaxing on my part (and courage on their part) but finally they gave a definite answer to my question. The children watched 3½ hours per day and even more on the weekends.

After expressing some surprise and alarm, I suggested that they gather their children together and announce new rules governing the TV, specifically that they be allowed to see no more than thirty minutes of a parent-authorized, pre-selected program each day.

Do you remember those pictures of the first atomic bombs? Well, imagine *two* of them going off at the same time—in my study. These shaken parents were already forming pictures of three more mega-bombs exploding right on their living room floor when they made the announcement to their children.

What had happened was that we had bumped up against the awesome power of three very strong children. Through the years, and quite unconsciously, the parents had let the power to control their home life slip out of their hands into the hands of their children. The parents correctly gauged that to take back that power now might have an effect similar to throwing gasoline on a fire.

A bit later, I'll tell you what actually happened with the power in this family.

I want to give one more illustration of power in the hands of young children.

A good friend of mine, who is a seventh grade science teacher, recently told me that there is a new kind of threat which twelve-year-olds now make to their teachers. In the heat of conflict, a student will seriously shout at the teacher: "I'm going to *sue* you!" This is no small weapon because the parents almost invariably take the side of the student against the teacher.

My teacher friend has a most happy response to such an assault.

Power in Young Children

Taking the student aside, he positions himself squarely in front of the student, nose to nose, and announces, "You just go right ahead and sue me. That's perfectly okay. You know why? Because I already have the best lawyer in town and if you sue me we are going to give you such a fight in court that you'll be forever sorry you stepped into the courtroom. In addition to that, I know the judge and he *hates* kids messing around his courtroom. Now—are we going to do it my way, or do you want trouble?"

Then the teacher waits. He waits patiently until the power is back in his hands. That may take some time because children are tenacious and brutally strong. There is no alternative, however, to simply waiting until the misbehaving student conforms to the will of the teacher. In the old days, a teacher could spank the child. This was a convincing way of hastening the conformity of the student. It was marvelously efficient in helping the student make up his mind. Today, however, spanking is forbidden. This leaves the teacher with no alternative except to patiently wait out the student until the power is once again in his hands.

A number of things come to mind as I reflect on the three examples above. They are very instructive.

In the episode at the supermarket where the child got her candy bar, we see power wholly in the hands of the child. The mother's delimitation of that power was half-hearted, weak and, I feel, tragic. Mother allowed herself to be run down by a four-year-old Mack truck. The best mother could do was extract a weak promise from her daughter to be "good"—whatever that meant.

The responsibility for this tragedy, of course, must rest wholly on the mother. She allowed it to happen, step by step. She could have stopped the conversation and the actions at any point. I, for one, had hoped that she would have slapped her daughter's hand, firmly replaced the candy bar on the rack and told the child to be quiet. Mother, however, chose to take the easy route. She allowed herself to be the weak one and her four-year-old the highest power in this interpersonal transaction. By this means, the mother was teaching her daughter that her authorities can be dominated if only one

11

exercises sufficient power. "Might makes right." Whence does this power come? From two sources: (1) the natural omnipotential thinking of the child and (2) the weakness of human authorities.

Turning now to the second example—the parents who restricted the use of the TV from 3½ hours to thirty minutes per day. Once again we see defaulting parents. Power in the family had been picked up by the children—at least, so it seemed to the parents. But there was another factor at work in the children on which the parents had not counted: fatigue. The children, understandably, were tired of TV and almost welcomed the opportunity to turn away from this daily tiring, lengthy, empty encounter with the idiot box! Good kids!

When the parents laid down the thirty minute rule for TV, they expected a battle to take place on that issue. The children, in this instance, decided that the battlefield was not worth defending. All that there was left for me to do with these parents was to assure them that there would be other battlefields where the issue of power would indeed be fought out.

The final example I used was the science teacher who was threatened with a lawsuit by his student. The teacher, you recall, met this threat with the threat of superior power—and the pretense of welcoming such an encounter.

If my understanding is correct, this teacher did exactly what should be done in such a situation. The teacher refused to be intimidated. He insisted he had superior power because of his role as teacher and that it was the task of his student to come to terms with that power. Such a position was good for the teacher and good for the student.

It was to the credit of the student that he made a verbal threat rather than pulling a knife on the teacher. Had that happened, the teacher would have been wise to indicate, in every way, that there was to be no contesting the student's power. Teachers, like parents, cannot win every battle. It's all right, sometimes, to be powerless.

The position I have taken above is in sharp contradiction to a very strong philosophy of child-rearing which is currently sweeping our country. The movement is called Parent Effectiveness Training or P.E.T. Dr. Thomas Gordon, a psychologist, is the guiding spirit behind this movement. Training sessions in P.E.T. are widely offered, often under the sponsorship of churches, and the basic text has already gone through many printings.

Parent Effectiveness Training bears directly on our subject. I will sketch, first, how P.E.T. views a child and, secondly, how P.E.T. suggests a parent function with his child.

A child, according to Dr. Gordon, must from earliest childhood learn to manage his own life. He must learn to be the manager of his feelings, and, please, let no parent interfere with an evaluation of those feelings! The child will evaluate his own feelings and eventually set the limits of his own behavior. A child has a right to feel as he wishes, and, if only the parents will stop resisting this growth process in the child, he will eventually become an autonomous person. Most parents, however, "depend on a method used 2,000 years ago."

If, for example, your young son walks up to you and kicks you in the shin, you are not to respond with either rebuke or punishment. You are not even supposed to stop him! P.E.T. urges you to respond with: "Ouch! That really hurt me. I don't like to be kicked." The purpose of such a response is to refrain from an externally imposed discipline and encourage the child to be *self*-disciplined. When the child is made aware of the results of his behavior (pain in your shin), he is expected to correct himself. A parent only interrupts and damages this growth process by a message to the child that he is wrong and should change his behavior. Children need an unencumbered freedom to grow—and they will grow up straight only if parents will not interfere with that growth. "If parents could learn only one thing from this book", writes Dr. Gordon, "I wish it were this: each and every time they force a child to do something by their power and authority, they deny that child a chance to learn self-discipline and self-responsibility."

Of what use, then, are parents?

In addition to really listening to the child and accepting him just as he is, P.E.T. teaches that the parent can be a model; he can be a consultant to the child; he can develop a loving relationship with the child. Most importantly, however, the parent must never use his power on the child. A parent uses power on a child when he sets standards and limits, insists upon compliance, and follows through with punishment if the child disobeys. The use of parental power, according to P.E.T., actually produces adolescent rebellion and eventually adult neurosis. It is unethical, claims Dr. Gordon, for parents to bully their children with their superior power. Therefore parents should abandon its use. Failure to do so will only confirm that ignorant parents—*not* the children—are the problem.

According to P.E.T., once coercive tactics have been abandoned by the parents, they can be trained to handle situations of conflict with their children by means of negotiation and arbitration, each party being equal to the other. Neither child nor parent can have his own way unless it is agreeable to the other.

People who believe in P.E.T. recommend this kind of negotiation because they claim no one wins and no one loses. But is that true? No—it is false because the authority-bearers not only default in the proper and beneficial use of their authority, but in addition, the egocentrism of the child goes unchallenged. From my point of view, P.E.T. recommends a consistently soft love, whereas I am recommending tough love in disciplinary problems.

Dr. Gordon, in his book *Parent Effectiveness Training*, shares many enthusiastic reports of parents who have suddenly seen the error of their ways, begun to use the P.E.T. methods, and now report a completely changed home life. Many children are also enthusiastic about what P.E.T. has done for their parents. The children tangibly express their gratitude with new cooperation and affection.

Small wonder!

When parents renounce their power and return to the level of their children, can we expect anything else than rejoicing; the parents for the return of domestic peace and the children for the freedom to get things their own way?

Someday, however, both parent and child will understand that they were self-deceived. They will know that the price of such a mistake, when the spoiled child becomes an unchallenged, egocentric adult, is terrible suffering and heartache.*

At this point, something must be said about child abuse.

Child abuse is usually an instance where the power of the child is pitted against the superior power of a parent. Both of them are using power wrongly. The child often refuses to be obedient to the parent. The parent certainly refuses to be limited by God. Both child and parent presume to have unlimited power. It is a situation which cries out for obedience to authority. The law correctly holds the parent responsible for physical harm to the child, even though the child is insubordinate.

The whole situation must be remedied quickly by submission to Highest Power—the child to his parent and the parent to God. If this does not happen, not only will the child be seriously injured, but the sins of the parent will surely be upon the children for generations to come, for the Lord visits "the iniquity of the fathers upon the children to the third and fourth generation of those who hate me" (Exodus 20:5). Egocentric behavior in one generation has a way of teaching that very philosophy of life to future generations. This is a valid negative reason for a parent to change his behavior. There is also a positive reason: God shows his steadfast love unto "thousands of those who love me and keep my commandments."

A child-abusing parent has it in his hands to solve both his problem and his child's problem by the simple device of radical obedience to God. Each new generation of fathers and mothers need desperately to learn this good news. This learning must begin with the parents. They must be the first to learn radical obedience to God, lest they harm the precious children God has entrusted to them. Child abuse is basically a parental problem—one which cries out for solution through the cries and moans of their hospitalized children.

---

* This material on P.E.T. appeared as a magazine article in the *Church Herald* on July 25, 1975. It is used by permission.

3

Power Among Adolescents

Most of the current literature on adolescent behavior, I feel, has a deep error at its very heart.

The error is this, that the *parents,* rather than the child, are the ones who are expected to change their ideas and behavior.

This is the very thing we noticed with Parent Effectiveness Training. It is always the parents who are asked to make the changes, not the child. It is a mistake for parents, we are told, to take a position and expect the child to come to terms with it. This theme also runs through the entire secular, psychological literature dealing with adolescence. Parents must make the changes—not their children—because parents are almost invariably doing the wrong thing.

It takes no special discernment to see that such a position is a destructive attack upon authority and Highest Power. So long as the authority-bearers (parents) are constantly changing their minds, they are exceedingly difficult to pin down, and almost impossible to obey. Since obedience is a bad word both to teenagers and secular, humanistic psychologists, it follows that they will both strongly argue for changes in the authority-bearer and a non-judgmental acceptance of the adolescent's behavior.

I have before me a representative magazine article on adolescence, written by a Christian psychologist. I am sure the man is a Christian, but when he talks psychology, he sounds pagan to me. At some length, he notes the defensiveness of parents and their denial of reality. Parents, he continues, fail to really listen to their children.

And, during this "time of fragile self-esteem for the adolescent," parents must learn to be non-judgmental. In this vein, he goes on to say how parents, not the adolescent, must do the changing.

The reason parents willingly change themselves rather than their adolescent child is simply because most parents are afraid of the power their children wield. We can only guess as to how this sad situation has come to be. It was not that the parents were lazy or did not care. The problem went deeper. It had to do with the parents' unfinished business from their own childhood. If the issue of authority was indecisively dealt with in their lives, there is little hope that they can now be stable authorities in the lives of their children.

When the wild, unharnessed egocentrism of the adolescent smashes into weak, defaulting parents, the results are unpleasantly predictable. The parents are bowled over and the adolescent again has what he has always been after from the beginning of his life—power.

This explains, too, why adolescents resort to drugs and alcohol. These chemicals are quick trips to power. The "high" experienced is a sensation of well-being because of power. The user says to himself: "Everything is going to be all right," because he feels on top of situations in his life. There are plenty more sophisticated explanations of why people use drugs and alcohol, but none so illuminating as power.

Now no one questions the fact that, as an adolescent gets older, the parental restraints must be progressively relaxed. What is important is that this process take place out of the strength of the parents, rather than their weakness. This means that the parents consciously choose to diminish their supervision of their adolescent. It also means that when the inevitable conflicts of adolescents arise, the parents calmly prevail, even if it means calling in the strong arm of the law to keep the peace.

I recall the case of a seventeen-year-old girl who was in rebellion against her parents. The girl threatened to run away. Finally, in the heat of a battle with her parents, the girl actually did leave the house and took off down a lonely, rural road late at night.

Her parents were very wise. They did a very loving thing for their daughter. They called the police and asked to have her returned home. The policemen gladly complied. They quickly understood their function: to give a show of superior power to an egocentric adolescent intent on having her own way.

The policemen placed the young lady safely in the back seat of the squad car, declining to offer any information to her. She cooperated, feeling sure that her parents would take her side and defend her against these terrible policemen.

Upon returning home, the daughter soon learned that her parents had *called* the police and were in full support of what they had done! This caused momentary bitterness until she clearly understood that both authorities—parents and police—stood solidly against her. Such opposition was too much. She backed down, cooled off and became obedient.

This episode also illustrates a fundamental rule with adolescents. It is the *behavior* we want changed, not the feelings, nor the understanding. The parents and the police wanted only that that adolescent girl bring her body home. She could feel as she wished. She could have whatever understanding of the situation she wished to have. But she *had* to come home.

As the adolescent person enters adulthood, no matter how effective and loving his parents have been, we can be fairly sure that the Kingdom of Self is nonetheless solidly established. This is a kingdom in rebellion to the Kingdom of God. There is conflict between these two kingdoms as to which holds the highest power.

In future days, we will see open warfare between these contending authorities. More often, the egocentric king or queen will construct an elaborate facade made out of good intentions, pseudo-morality and dead religion.

The God of *all* power, however, has His own plans for each beloved child. He knows we are in a prison of our own device and that we have thrown the key away. As a grieving Father searching for His lost children, God searches out the dark dungeons of the earth. In His hand He holds a master key. It is the key to life and freedom.

4

Power in Marriage

When a man and a woman marry, they join two power systems. By that I mean that each party brings to the wedding service a highly complex mechanism whereby each has learned to control his world. This mechanism, in each party, has through the years been tested, altered and even redesigned many times. The young man and young woman assume that, upon marriage, these two autonomous power systems will blend and work together. They are sure that their love for each other is strong enough to do this.

This *should* be the case, but it seldom is. What actually happens is that, as soon as the marriage vows are spoken, the contest of power begins. To our amazement and horror, we see young marrieds using their power upon each other. It just seems to be a fact that people have enough egocentrism in them to want to fight, much more than to love, each other. Wedding bells signal the official beginning of what will surely turn out to be a power struggle lasting, in some cases fifty or sixty years.

Sometime ago I married a couple who were very much in love before their wedding. As they left for the honeymoon, however, they got into a terrible fight in their car. It seemed the young man had on one of his older suits. The new bride was infuriated. Why had he not bought a new suit? Why was he so tight-fisted with money? And was this the way their marriage was going to be?

Happily, for the first few days of marriage, most married people dream the same dreams, form the same goals, sleep in the same bed, enjoy a beautiful relationship. Each tries hard to please the other. But if often happens that husband and wife soon find themselves locked in a serious power struggle—and both mean business! Neither has any intention of losing the fight. Each is aware that there is going to be one winner and one loser in this marriage. Both have appointed themselves the winner.

When a husband tries to prevail over his wife, we can call it "god-playing." Similarly, when a wife tries to prevail over her husband, we can call it "goddess-playing." What happens in marriage is that *both* parties in their struggle for power do the wrong thing at the same time—the one in action, the other in reaction. What we see, therefore, is a god and a goddess locked in an extended, intense power struggle.

Right at this point, we can appreciate the fact that many marriages are not working well, simply because there is an intense struggle for power constantly going on between husband and wife. This often causes a great deal of marital pain.

Marital pain is everywhere in evidence in our society. Some friends recently asked me, "Is *anybody* happy today? We know of so few happy couples." These are indeed hard days for every married couple—unless the power problem is solved decisively, once and for all.

There are at least four faulty, and therefore, painful arrangements of power in marriage.

1. *The dictatorial god and the resentful goddess.*

This kind of marriage is one in which the husband, early in the marriage, collects all the power he can lay his hands on. Thereafter he quickly makes almost all the decisions, usually without even consulting his wife.

Eric is a good example of a dictatorial god.

Even before marriage, Eric set his wife straight about how things would go regarding religion in their marriage. He insisted that they be married by his priest, at his church, even though Thelma was a Protestant. Thelma protested at first, but Eric was adamant.

Power in Marriage

Soon after marriage, money problems arose. Eric earned a good wage as a carpenter, but the couple had to stick to a fairly strict budget. It was agreed that Thelma would have a fixed amount every week for food. All went well for a month, but then Eric began to have second thoughts about the amount budgeted for food. Thelma was bringing home what he considered to be the wrong kind of food—certain junk foods, expensive pecans and out-of-season fruits. Eric was not slow in bringing this to the attention of Thelma. He announced that he would cut her budget allotment if she continued to misuse it.

And then there was a problem with the use of vacation time. Eric was a deer hunter who felt he had a divine right to a week with his friends during deer season. Thelma was agreeable only because she hoped that, at another time, she might decide where to spend a second week of their vacation. At an appropriate time, she broached the matter—with disastrous results. They had a terrible fight which ended with Thelma once again backing down. But this time there was a difference. She vowed to herself that somehow, some way, she would get even with this man who was "squeezing the breath out of me."

Eric noticed that Thelma was changing her attitude toward him. She was far less responsive sexually. And she had less to say. Conversations were short and business-like. They were soon eating their meals either in silence or while watching TV. Eric made some effort to make conversation, but it was obvious that Thelma was slipping away from him.

What we see with Eric and Thelma is a marriage of a dictatorial god and a resentful goddess.

Eric, a forceful person who had always liked the feel of power in relationships, quickly took charge of the power in his marriage.

Thelma, who at one time admired Eric's ability to take charge, later came to resent him deeply. She now hated the very quality she had once admired in him. She knew that the resentment was burning a hole in her because she found herself plotting ways to get back at her husband.

From Eric and Thelma we can learn that the dictatorial god is like a man who builds a beautiful home only to watch helplessly as his resentful goddess causes it to go up in flames. Thelma has not yet set the fire. In time, however, her resentment will take the form of destructive deeds against her husband.

Both Eric and Thelma are using power on each other. There is great danger that both will suffer, for the price of using power in marriage is the destruction of both love and the marriage.

2. *The cruel god and the doormat goddess.*

Power in a husband can quickly take the form of cruelty toward his wife. Examples are easy to find. Let us look at Max and Helen, a middle-aged couple.

Max was a Marine in World War II. Ever since, he has tried to project an image of toughness and daring. It is very important to him to be seen as a strong, devil-may-care roughneck. One day, at a family picnic, Max took hold of their dog and said, "Want to see how President Johnson lifted up his dog?" With that, he took the heavy animal and lifted him by the ears. The poor dog howled in pain as he raced away from Max. Some of the family members tried to laugh it off but others remarked sadly about Max's cruel streak.

Unfortunately, this sadistic tendency also showed up in the marriage. Max had a nasty habit of putting Helen down in the presence of their friends. This was easy to do because Helen had a strong faith in God and liked the company of Christian friends. They had something going called a "prayer chain" in which one person would inform the others of a particular pressing need so that all could pray about it. Max seldom missed an opportunity to register his amusement with the prayer chain. Whenever a problem presented itself, Max would loudly announce to all, "It's time to give a little jerk to that prayer chain again."

Max had still other ways of getting to Helen.

He did it with a crude sexual interest in other women. Max missed few opportunities to examine and comment upon the anatomy of other women, all for the ears of Helen. He told her over and over again that such interest was normal, innocent and even helpful to his sexual interest in her. Helen was particularly vulnerable on the matter of sex because of her weight problem. She was obsessed with jealousy, not to mention anger and rage toward Max. More than once it broke out into a physical battle with Helen pummelling Max. He seemed to enjoy this: trading blows with an opponent was a language he well understood.

Thre is one more thing you need to know about Max: he was fascinated with pornography. Early in the marriage, Max kept it a poorly guarded secret, but a dozen years ago, he boldly laid a copy of *Playboy* on the coffee table. Helen never liked it but tolerated the competition. Later, however, she came to regret her tolerance. Max tested her further with a suggestion that he rent a few movies from the local adult book store. Helen exploded and barred the movies. But the marriage was now in shambles.

This is the story of Max, a cruel god, but also of Helen, who became a doormat goddess (by which I mean that her reaction was very passive and self-destructive). Helen now began to eat—with a vengeance. All ability to control food left her as resentment consumed her. She further insulated her life from Max by turning to her religious friends. They understood her. They accepted her.

The last I heard of Helen, she was still a strong link in the prayer chain. But I often wonder if these prayer chains are ever used for the members themselves. Self-destructive Helen needs it as much as cruel Max.

So far, we have examined two examples of the marriage of a powerful god and the reactions of the goddess. Now, with two more examples, we turn to the goddess as the active agent with power in marriage and the reaction of the god.

3. *The usurping goddess and the defaulting god.*
Let me tell you about Barbara and Ben.

When I label Barbara a usurping goddess, I simply mean that she, taking power from a husband who refuses to play his rightful role in marriage, plays the role for him. This all began ten years ago on the day they got married.

I happen to know the pastor who married them. He told me that, an hour before the wedding ceremony was to begin, Barbara came to his office in a panic. She had an urgent question about the wedding liturgy which she had somehow forgotten to ask during pre-marital counseling. "Are you going to ask me to *obey* my husband after we are married?" she asked anxiously.

The pastor—a real people-pleaser rather than a man of God— assured her that the form did not use the word *obey* and that, although she would be asked to be subject to her husband, it was intended to be a mutual subjection of both parties to each other.

The answer soothed Barbara. Her power was preserved.

I am happy to say that the marriage went tolerably well for the first few months. But then some changes began to take place in Barbara. She began to be bored with her marriage. She decided to get a job. Once she began working she noted an immediate improvement in her mood. In fact, she felt better at work than anywhere! Working made her feel alive. It also made her busier. Ben cooperated by taking her out to eat two or three times a week. He also became an expert operator of the vacuum cleaner.

Both Barbara and Ben liked having the extra income that Barbara's job provided. Barbara was better with figures than Ben, so she wrote the checks and generally controlled the budget. She also had a few envelopes, unknown to Ben, in which she would secretly stash away money for her special projects.

Barbara was a very busy woman but somehow she took the time to bear two children, a boy who is now seven and a girl who is five. Each child was placed with a baby-sitter or in a nursery school as soon as possible so Barbara could return to work. She was extremely busy. To her credit, she *cared* about her kids. Indeed, the truth is that she *lived* for them. With such a strong commitment, it is understandable that the disciplining of the children came to rest increasingly in her hands rather than Ben's.

Now in their tenth year of marriage, it is obvious that Barbara has in several ways become its leader. Feminism has had a strong impact upon her thinking, even causing her to seriously consider running for political office. The words *assertive* and *combative* are not too strong to describe her personality. These very qualities became something of a problem in the marriage in which Ben is increasingly passive and unexpressive. He seldom speaks and when he does, he is very careful with what he says. "To tell the truth," Ben confided in me, "I'm afraid of her most of the time."

The last detail of interest to us in this marriage is Ben's growing problem of impotence. Their physician is now arranging for them to see a sex therapist for help with this problem.

Ben and Barbara are a classic example of the usurping goddess and the defaulting god.

Most American marriages today are being shaped into this pattern. It is a painful, sick arrangement, both unworthy and destructive to human beings. The distribution of power is painfully wrong and badly needs correction. Which is to say, too, that there is still much hope for such marriages, as we will see later.

6. The prima donna goddess and the spectator god.

Let us look at the lives of Donna and Don who are both in their mid thirties.

Donna is a trim, fashionable woman who quickly attracts attention. I will never forget when she came to my wife and me for counseling. At one point in the session, she rose dramatically from her chair and began pacing the room as she talked and gestured. I thought it rather odd behavior. Then it dawned on me that this woman had made a theater out of my study. She was now putting on a little show for us. Donna was the star.

Most star performers have large wardrobes and Donna was no exception. She loved clothes and bought the newest designer fashions. Don had the kind of income which could cover Donna's clothing bills but he had lately begun complaining because she was obviously a compulsive buyer. She admitted that this was true. But how could she stop? She couldn't resist the temptation to buy all those clothes. Fortunately, I had a suggestion ready. I suggested as a starter that she turn her credit cards over to her husband. My good idea was promptly acknowledged and just as promptly ignored. Then she began a monologue on her problematic husband.

"He leaves much to be desired," she explained. "I'm getting awfully tired of giving, giving, *giving* with so little return. I admit I'm no angel—especially when I'm angry and begin throwing things—but when will this man begin doing his job as a husband to me and a father to his children? Maybe I should not compare him with my father, but I sure wish Don would go to him for a few lessons on how to play the male role."

I interrupted to ask if Don loved her.

"He loves me but he does not like me. He likes other woman, though when I accuse him of it he denies it."

One thing that Donna cannot deny, however, is Don's sensitivity and understanding of her chronic back injury. Donna has suffered— but not silently!—for many years with this problem. Don has yet to utter a word of complaint. He faithfully takes her for chiropractic treatments each week. The problem has also been a strain on their sexual life but, once again, Don has been both patient and understanding. He finds an odd but real satisfaction in faithfully taking care of Donna with this undeniable affliction. "The show," as they are both accustomed to say to each other, "must go on!"

And it does. Donna is the prima donna. Don is the spectator.

Come back with me to take another look at a baby.

A baby is a nearly perfect god-player. It is difficult for us to really understand that because we think of a child as being small, limited, undeveloped, helpless. In many ways he is just that. As far as his power goes, however, he is already a giant. He wants what he wants. He is fiercely determined to get it.

Wise parents understand that the child's power must be broken. They correctly observe that giving in to a child yields only a temporary peace which is soon broken by yet more and greater demands on the parents. In this contest of wills and power, effective parents insist that they win.

But they do not!

I'll tell you why.

First, nobody's perfect. Even wise, effective parents have weak-nesses, inconsistencies, differences between each other and, not least, often suffer from sheer fatigue. The young child will often get his way for no other reason than that the parents are too tired to stop him.

Secondly, our young egoist will many times be in situations where he is on his own, doing his own thing with only limited restriction. He may have things his way as he plays alone in the backyard. Place a few more children in the backyard, and he may soon emerge as "king of the mountain." If he fails to achieve that goal today, he will secretly plot to get control of his uncooperative playmates.

Finally, children are winners in situations where certain adults give children what the parents deny. When I was very young, I loved to go to grandma's house for supper. Grandma always had a Dutch sinterklaas cookie for me to eat while she was preparing the meal. It was all the more delicious because my mother had a strict rule at home against cookies before supper. What could I do but eat it, since mother was not there to stop me?

The point I am making is that children, in spite of even heroic parental control, come out as winners in the battle for power.

The problem only gets worse in the period of youth and adolescence. The Kingdom of Self grows steadily. No sacrifice is too great to make this kingdom work. Massive efforts are gladly made to convey the impression that "I have arrived," that "I am in control of myself," that "I am unique." Would that each egocentric would stop right there and be content with his achievement! He goes on, however, to assert that "I am prepared to match my power against others in the hope that I will emerge as a leader!" Is not that the secret prayer offered by every high school and college graduate?

While all that is taking place in this person's head, some other things are going on sexually. The day of sexual maturity has arrived and the time has come to seek a mate for marriage. Driven by overwhelming sexual desire and led by an idyllic fantasy of marital bliss, two people eventually, for better or worse, meet in a church to make their marriage vows.

Little do they realize that these vows are God's unique signal that He will now begin to shatter their respective power systems so that they may find Him as the Highest Power. How does he do this? God established marriage as His way of getting two of His children to fully display the worst in themselves—their egocentrism. A merciful, loving Father cares very much that all this unfinished business having to do with power and authority, be decisively dealt with and put to rest.

I have already described in some detail four basic types of marriages in which we could clearly see what happens when a man and a woman join their power systems in marriage. It can safely be said that *every* marriage begins with a bad power adjustment between husband and wife. Each one's commitment to power is so deep and extensive that a marital contest is inevitable. As in all two-person contests, there is only one winner and one loser. The effort to win, therefore, is total. And, on the part of the "loser," there is usually total resentment.

Once the powers are firmly joined in a protracted marital struggle, something else occurs. The marriage flies out of control. In this difficult and dangerous time, one party goes out of control with a nervous breakdown, uncontrolled drinking, obesity, dependency on various drugs, etc., or, more actively, physical struggle, child abuse, verbal attacks, infidelity, etc. When a person exhibits such dire signs of lack of control he may want very much to be in control of himself. But this proves to be impossible. Sincere resolutions, promises, even vows do not stop such behavior. There is a simple inexorable law at work at this stage of the marriage and it reads as follows:

> He who tries to be in control
> must fly out of control
> until he comes
> under Control.

When the controls of a person are no longer working for whatever reason, it is certainly understandable (though not permissible) that his mind turn to death as a solution to the problem. Marital pain does that, for no other kind of pain compares with it in intensity.

The death-desire may go either in the direction of divorce (the death of the marriage) suicide or homicide, or both. All of these options are immoral and sinful. Yet, if the marriage is to live again, something in it must die.

Power in Marriage

What?

Power must die preferably in both husband and wife, but if not in both, then in one party. For human power, unsubmitted to Divine Power, is *supposed* to die. It is a good death. Let it die, for human power has the potential to kill both the marriage and the persons involved in it.

Human power dies only when it is submitted to Divine Power. This is abundantly taught in the Scriptures. "He who loses his life for my sake will find it" (Matt. 10:39). "I am crucified with Christ: nevertheless I live; yet not I, but Christ liveth in me" (Gal. 2:20). "For while we live, we are always being given up to death for Jesus' sake" (2 Cor. 4:11). These precious passages encourage us to die to our self-life and live under and out of Divine Power.

Beware of solutions to marital problems which propose less drastic solutions. There are all kinds of counselors around who are offering cheap "solutions" which are unworthy of suffering people. Some of my colleagues in the ministry are pitifully weak and unhelpful when they explain marital conflict as simply a problem of "not being able to really communicate with each other." Another pastor blandly tells married couples to "each give one hundred percent to the marriage." Bleeding, dying marriages need much more than these little Band-aids of popular psychology.

A week ago, Ed and Susan came to our home. We knew them when they were unmarried, living together and expecting a child. It was during those days that Susan went after Ed with a knife and Ed was full of drugs. We got Susan into a maternity home for unwed mothers. She broke every rule in the place and got thrown out.

But a week ago they both returned. They had gotten married and were completely changed! How had it happened? Ed said, "It all began to happen here two years ago—in your study—when you explained what living to self was doing to us and you asked us both to surrender our lives to Jesus Christ. We did not know the meaning of what we were doing then, but God did. He is now the Power in our lives!"

God is the Highest Power.
Husband and wife are to be subordinate to Him.

31

God, however, has added one more rule: wives are to be in subjection to their husbands. Read Titus 2:5; 1 Cor. 14:34, 35; Eph. 5:22-24.

So let us ask two simple questions:

1. What does it mean for a husband, that his wife be in subjection to him?

2. What does it mean for a wife to allow her husband to make the final decisions?

1. What does it mean for a husband, that his wife be in subjection to him?

A. It means that he *love* her, love her even more than himself with all his male ego. True love for a wife seeks what is good for her. A loving husband treats his wife kindly and with patience. He quickly forgives her faults and extols her strengths and virtues. A husband's love is quick to defend his wife, often against her own children. This kind of man speaks well of her in public.

B. It means that the husband realize that he, too, is a person under authority, in this case, authority of the Lord. Such a man understands that there is no place in his role as husband for a tyrannical, authoritarian attitude. He, too, is under authority.

It follows that he is never to force or coerce his wife to obey him. Getting married is not like joining the army. In the army, if a soldier refuses to take orders in battle, he is court-martialed and punished. Wives are not soldiers. They cannot be forced, nor should they be brought to court.

In situations where the differences are not reconcilable, no action is to be taken. A good husband will, in such a situation, try to negotiate a solution suitable to both husband and wife. This leads to my third point.

C. It means that a husband *listen* to his wife. Husbands should be eager to learn from their wives. In many areas, her fund of knowledge and experience is greater than her husband's. A wife should never hold back in offering suggestions, reactions to what her husband says, and new ideas to her husband. She may suggest what she thinks the final decision should be, but then, if she is really wise, she will

32

draw back and encourage her husband to come to his own conclusions.

D. Since the husband, according to the Christian model of marriage, is called upon to make final decisions, it follows that he must bear ultimate responsibility for his decisions. He can, in no circumstances, fault his wife for a wrong decision.

E. The submission of a wife to her husband means, finally, that the husband exclude their children from the decision-making process. The process of decision-making is sufficiently complicated with husband and wife as participants. I think it is important to hear and collect the feelings and ideas of the children, but their contributions are definitely to be subordinate to their mother's and under no circumstances should children intrude into the decision-making process of both parents.

2. What does it mean for a wife to allow her husband to make the final decisions?

A. That she learn to obey—graciously—even when the decision of her husband is against her desires. I realize how abhorrent this is to the modern mind and the cause of feminism, but I offer to you the testimony of hundreds of women whom I know, who gladly testify to the fact that this kind of marriage not only *works* but brings the most *satisfaction*.

There is only one time that a wife may disobey her husband. She should disobey him in that normally rare instance when her husband asks her to do something immoral or illegal.

It may happen. I knew a husband who told his wife to shop-lift an item in the grocery store. I knew another husband who told his wife to write a bad check. Such instances, however, are relatively rare.

Normally, husband and wife differ in *matters of judgment*. A wife may sincerely believe, in such cases, that her opinion is better and wiser than her husband's. In a Christian marriage, however, the answer is clearly spelled out in Scripture. A wife is to obey her husband in all things lawful.

B. Christian marriage means that a wife support and encourage her husband in his difficult role as leader in the marriage. Clear signals of support and encouragement from the wife to the husband are especially needed in this sick, American culture in which many husbands have become weak, passive and servile.

C. A woman in submission to her husband will function as head of the home in the absence of her husband. When he returns, however, the final power must again revert back to him. This is a difficult transition, as several wives of career military servicemen have told me. When the husband returns, after a prolonged absence, it is very difficult for such a wife to relinquish her position of highest power in the home. But it must be done.

D. For a wife, submission in marriage means that she freely disclose to her husband, the full range of her understandings, insights and wisdom. She is to be completley frank, open and honest with him. He needs such input, along with his own understandings, to come to good and wise decisions.

E. Finally, a wife, under no circumstances, should ever side with her children against her husband. It often happens in the marriages I see. Many a wife loves her children far more than her husband, and it will always show in the decision-making process, to the detriment of all.

The God-dominated marriage, with strong male leadership and submissive female support, is one in which the issue of power is settled. All power belongs to God. He, who made us and redeemed us, also knows how to make our marriages work. They work beautifully when the power issue is settled in favor of God, and we play the scriptural roles He has assigned to us.

Such a marriage is one of God's most beautiful creations.

5

Power in the Family

There is a game we all play from the day we are born to the day we die. The name of the game is *power*.

But no one tells us that *that* is the game, nor does anyone tell us the *name* of the game. It is the purpose of this book to enlighten us on both scores.

Enough has been said about the struggle for power between parents and their children. I want to say something now about the child and his siblings.

Psychologists and psychiatrists have been trying for years to discover the secrets of what is called the family constellation. What are the usual characteristics of the first child? What causes the pairing of some children to the exclusion of others? Why is one child somehow elected to be the "sick one" of the family? Why do some families have one who is the "escapee"? What are the characteristics of the last child? Can any principles or laws be discerned? Can we make any predictions about the future stance of the children in a family? And, can young parents do anything to prevent future trouble? These are a few of the questions thoughtful people have asked.

Unfortunately, there are still no answers to these questions.

I doubt if we ever will have answers on the basis of which we can make predictions about each family member. The hereditary and environmental factors are so multitudinous and unique in the case of each family member that no honest researcher can hope to make any reliable predictive statement.

POWER GREATER THAN OURSELVES

The best we can do, perhaps, is to look back on a family which God has providentially raised up and learn, by hindsight, what has happened. Look with me, for a few moments, at what happened in a particular family of five children.

Albert, the eldest son, was father's special boy. From childhood, he wanted to be like father. That meant that he "played" father with the growing family. When the family was at the table, Albert would control the four younger children with commands he knew would please father.

The second son, Brad, was always close to Albert. They got along surprisingly well simply because Brad's personality complemented Albert's. Brad was warm and kind. Albert was haughty and detached. Somehow they seemed to fit and, though many years have passed, they still see each other often.

The Albert-Brad partnership was not opened to include the third member of the family, particularly because she was a girl. Cynthia always seemed drawn to the world outside her family. During the 1930s, she was deeply interested in movies, dancing, art, travel. She could not wait to leave home and get away from a family she regarded as narrow and provincial. She found such an opportunity when a smooth-talking soldier swept her into a marriage that subsequently rudely awakened her to the world of reality.

The fourth child was a boy, David. David got parental attention by being chronically ill. He has been hospitalized twenty-three times so far in his life and he gives every appearance of gloriously carrying the burden of his illness into old age. He uses his "cross" to wield great power in the lives of many.

Finally, there is Evelyn, a very independent, self-sufficient family member. She was mother's special and last child. To the other children, she exposed no weakness, nor could anyone discern any of her deeper needs. She was a very private person in the family.

The dynamic at work in this family is power. Each one assumed a different posture, one which permitted some special access to one of the parents and some elevation over the other siblings.

Power in the Family

The problems with power in the family are seldom solved while the family is together. No child has ever received a satisfying amount of parental attention, nor is any child happy with his siblings, unless they are under his control. Even then, the egocentrism is so strong in the child that he invariably keeps his brothers and sisters under continual judgment. The passage of time seems to do nothing with these attitudes toward family. They just remain in a person and are added to the power-problems that invariably crop up in extra-family relationships.

A day will surely come, however, when God will sweep together all the accumulated rubbish of these unresolved power problems. The Lord is a concerned Home Owner who will sweep up all the old newspapers, junk, debris and dust in our lives and burn them. Yes! Each life is meant to come to a Great Resolution. The Answer to life arrives for each one of us on that day when the problem of power is put to rest by human powerlessness in the presence of the Omnipotent God.

Let us return for a moment to Albert, Brad, Cynthia, David and Evelyn. Mother is now deceased but father is still in reasonably good health.

The children must yet engage in one last and final contest of power. It will take place soon after father's death. The contest will decide who gets what of the family furniture, the jewelry, photographs, mementoes, mother's furs and even a little cash. We are happy that father has wisely drawn up a will which, thank the Lord, will divide the bank account. Even this prudent measure, however, holds the potential for a familial war because Albert, the executor of the will, intends to reimburse himself liberally for his professional services to the other family members.

It is in the distribution of the undesignated bequests—the furniture, jewelry, photos, mementoes and clothes I mentioned above—that the character of each surviving child will be tested. Each child will lay claim to as much as he can. Resentment will reign in each heart, even those who get the lion's share of the possessions. Children with the strongest wills will grab the most. Those who come away with little will shed tears of anger, complaining bitterly that, after forty years, nothing has changed in this family!

I sincerely hope that this final eruption of greed among the family members will not end in violence. I have personal knowledge of a family in which physical violence broke out between two brothers, both in their late fifties. This was a fist fight intended to determine one last time who had the most power. The fight between the two brothers ended in a draw and so the matter now rests in the hands of their lawyers.

What we are looking at in these cases of adult, parentless children, is a demonstration of raw power which has no limiting authority. All goes well when a father or mother makes a list of all their belongings, stating what each child is to receive. In such a case each member of the family takes comfort in the fact that, at least, he has not been swindled out of something by his sibling. Without a limiting authority, parentless children are doomed to a power struggle.

I must hastily add, however, that there is *one* important exception to this inevitable power struggle. The exception occurs when one of the children, having settled the issue of power in his life with God, no longer needs power. Once a person comes under His Power, there is no need to win the foolish games of human contest. A good example of this is found in the case of a man we will call Peter.

Peter, a brother and two sisters were gathered in the old homestead after their mother was buried. Father had long been dead. A dispute arose over the disposition of father's jewelry. Each brother stated his desire to have these mementoes, a few of them of some value.

Peter asserted his feelings but as soon as he was challenged by his brother, he declined to press for his "rights." It is true, Peter had as much right to the jewelry as his brother, but Peter also understood that there was something more important than the jewelry. Peter's *relationship* with his brother was the key issue. He understood that it was more important to have a good, loving relationship with his brother than a trinket of jewelry. Peter was sure that such was the will of God for him in this situation.

Every parent must surely hope for children such as Peter. I was recently told of an aged woman who, before she died, yearned to help her selfish, power-minded chidren through the difficult days following her death. Her solution to this problem was both simple and courageous.

She decided to take at least a good part of her money with her.

Her plans were carefully laid. At an advanced age, she converted much of her small estate to cash. These large bills she carefully concealed behind a framed picture of her husband who was already deceased. Verbal instructions were given to the children to place this picture in her coffin.

The plan almost worked. Unfortunately, one of her children—every family has a nosey spy—became suspicious and examined the picture of her father. When she did, and when she found the money, the faces of the weeping children were suddenly covered with smiles! "Mother tried to take it with her! Mother! Why would you do a thing like *that?* But mother, we love you the more for what you did!"

I was told that the cash was properly divided among the children, but I still feel badly about mother. Her children failed to learn the lesson she was trying to teach them. The lesson is this: the best thing to do with power (money is power) is to get rid of it!

6

Power in Emotional Illness

Every pastor has some special interest in his pastoral work. One friend of mine has a special interest in worship. Another is a specialist in Old Testament studies. I, too, have a field in the ministry which greatly interests me.

My speciality is to study and work with people who are breaking down with something called emotional illness. The Lord has given me an ideal place in which to study this problem: a state mental hospital. For the past twenty-five years, I have been sitting on the wards, talking and listening to people whose lives and personalities were coming apart.

In this chapter, I would like to rise from my chair after these twenty-five years of sitting, and come to a few conclusions about people who are emotionally ill. I want to share with you six conclusions.

1. The natural tendency of each person is to worship the delusion of himself as the Powerful One.

Let us look first at the well-known delusion of grandeur.

A number of my mental hospital friends have confided quite candidly to me that they are really someone other than they appear to be. One man said, "I may *look* like the man you know, but really I am God." Others may lay claim to being Napoleon, the Virgin Mary, Jesus, St. Paul or a great president.

POWER GREATER THAN OURSELVES

Why would the human mind drift in such a direction? The accepted answer in our society is that such minds are sick. I no longer believe that to be true.

Is it not a better explanation to understand that the identification of ourselves with certain grand personages is the simple attempt of an overloaded (and therefore weakened) mind to gain power? Anyone's mind, greatly fatigued over a long period of time, would begin to produce solutions to its suffering. How understandable that we desperately identify with a reincarnated powerful person or even with God Himself.

The over-fatigued or weakened mind may also identify with a peron like Adolf Hitler or even Satan. It makes little difference to a tired mind whether the person it anxiously identifies with is virtuous or evil. What counts is the power associated with the personage selected. Hitler had power, therefore the distressed mind may identify with him.

Delusions of grandeur, however, are only one type of delusion. There are many others. For our purposes, I want to lump four types of delusions together and deal with them as a whole. The delusions I have in mind are called:

(a) *Delusions of persecution* in which a person imagines that someone is bent on destroying his character or person.

(b) *Delusions of sin* in which a person is sure that he is responsible for committing some great sin, perhaps even the unpardonable sin. Sometimes such a person feels responsible for the sins of the whole world.

(c) *Delusions of jealousy* in which a person may fantasize, for example, that his marriage partner is unfaithful to him.

(d) *Delusions of disease* which usually has to do with imagined illnesses.

These delusions seem at first to be very different from the delusions of grandeur, which seemingly glorify the ego. The four delusions mentioned here seem to cause only suffering and pain. Is there any connection between these delusions? I think so.

We saw earlier that the "benefit" of a delusion of grandeur was the gaining of a sense of power. It made the person feel strong, usually as a compensation for undeniable weakness. It is this very same sense of power which is at work in the destructive delusions. Here, however, power is used to punish or even destroy. Unresolved guilt normally cries out for judgment upon the guilty one. The punishing delusion is one way we choose to again use power to straighten out our world and attempt to make sense of it.

2. Emotional illness is a sure-fire way to use power on family members.

When we consider emotional illness we are again looking at the action of raw power. Emotional illness has the effect of jerking other people around. So-called neurotic people are masters at setting up the whole family to contribute time, energy, sympathy and particularly money to the comfort and health of the neurotic member. One person I counseled put herself in the hospital fifteen times in one year.

An active alcoholic does the same thing with his drinking. The family is forced to give up money for alcohol. When the problem gets so bad that hospitalization is needed, the family must arrange for it. As soon as the alcoholic discovers that the accommodations and food are not to his liking, he will sign himself out and demand that his family transport him home. This is how a single "sick" person uses power on people to jerk them around.

3. When an emotionally ill person finally reaches out for counsel, he usually does so in the hope of increasing his power over an unmanageable world by means of the support and help of the counselor. He is not interested in making some needed changes in his life.

It took me several years to learn this. I once naively thought that people wanted to improve themselves and would listen to good reason and sound advice. Nonsense! Counselees continue to want what they have always wanted—power. They want the counselor to be supportive, non-judgmental, interested and especially smart so that he can give them what they really want; good tips on how better to succeed in the counselee's crazy world.

The only hope for such a person is that his cup of suffering may overflow. Intense, prolonged suffering can bring a person to a point of powerlessness. He loses control and hits bottom. Recovering alcoholics teach us that at that critical point, a person will either destroy himself or turn his life over to Higher Power. If a surrender is made to God, the problem of power is solved.

4. Most professional "help" offered to the emotionally ill worsens the condition of the suffering person. This is because the helpers cannot help but ignore the basic problem of egocentrism, that being their *own* unrecognized orientation.

Modern psychologists and psychiatrists see the emotionally ill person as courageously trying to fight his way into the human race. In their view his problems are caused by his immaturity. Therefore the last word or advice given to a troubled person is to *grow up.* Diagrammatically, it looks like this:

The emotionally ill person is thought to be "out in orbit." A resistive, often cruel environment of people (in the inner circle) have kept him from really joining the human race. Therefore, people and institutions in the inner circle are consistently faulted. Hopefully, the emotionally ill person, orphaned by a cruel world, will eventually find courage and opportunity to join the human race. To do this, he must be given a chance to grow up emotionally. Until then, he is immature.

Note that there is no place for God here because this diagram looks at life from a purely secular point of view.

Power in Emotional Illness

Please note that the above understanding of the human problem is the opposite of what I am suggesting in this book. In the first chapter, I tried to explain that the basic problem in life is that every person is born with a one-hundred percent commitment to himself as *the* central power in his world. Diagrammatically, he looks like this:

Other Human Beings

God is in exile because the Self occupies the place of God.

Looking at these two diagrams it is easy to see that the advice given by the non-Christian and the Christian counselor completely contradicts each other.

In Diagram A, the last word of the secular counselor to the counselee is *grow*—that is, grow up, do not be a child, stop being immature, begin to assert yourself, love yourself.

In Diagram B the last word of the Christian counselor to the counselee is *die*—die to your position as a god-player. Resign your position in the center, for it belongs to God; repent, confess your sin of self-idolatry and Godlessness.

If the suffering person, by the grace of God, can begin to die to self and live to God, a whole new world opens up to him.

In this magnificently simple way, God (not man) becomes the healer not only for the emotionally ill, but for us all. For we sin against God and the emotionally ill when we divide the human race into those who are healthy and those who are ill. (God-players always love to elevate themselves above their fellows and play the judge.)

45

POWER GREATER THAN OURSELVES

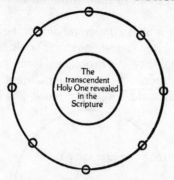

The position of the twice-born person.

The truth is that we are all sinners, equally in need of the saving grace of God. We are *all* sick and the sickness is called sin. The essence of sin is god-playing. None of us can save himself from such sin. The only help one sinner can give another is to point to their common Lord who will save them both.

5. The basic solution to our personal and inter-personal problems is a Person: God.

It is time for Christian believers to come right out and say that. Our help is not in man, not even *partly* in man. Salvation today, as it has always been, is from the Lord alone.

If that is true, then the very best counsel we can give to a suffering human being is to surrender his *person* and his *power* to God. Both the *gun* and the *ammunition* must be surrendered.

Our commitment to Self and Power, however, is so strong and deep that we will do almost anything to avoid a complete surrender. We give up only as little as we possibly can. Our commitment to Self is so tenacious that we will play silly games with God until new suffering drives us to a more complete surrender.

I am trying to describe here what life is all about. It is a series of increasingly more difficult deaths that the Self-life must undergo. It can also be a series of greater gifts of life from the endless bounty of Him who is life itself.

The great tragedy of our age is that people in emotional distress

46

cast aside the way of Jesus Christ and settle for the pseudo-help of humanism. Permit me to illustrate that statement.

In the psychological world, there are currently being practiced approximately 250 different psychotherapies. They range from psychoanalysis to behavior modification, from Rogerian therapy to transactional analysis. As I am now writing, the newest and latest offering is something called cognitive therapy. Cognitive therapy is used especially with depressed people. I refer to it here because it bears on our discussion and is also a prime example of yet another secular solution to emotional pain in people.

The central point of cognitive therapy is that negative thoughts are the cause of negative emotions which, in turn, produce depression. Our thoughts decree our moods. Therefore, if we think the right thoughts, we will avoid the suffering of depression. The federal government thinks so highly of this discovery that they have given 3.5 million dollars to the researchers who will now test the effectiveness of cognitive therapy.

In cognitive therapy, the patient is taught to recognize when he is experiencing self-defeating, negative thoughts about himself. As soon as he becomes aware of these mental saboteurs, he is to realize that (1) they are distortions and that (2) he is worthy of self-esteem. Yes, he is to remember that he is a person worthy of respect and honor. No more of that negative thinking. It is to be replaced with a judgment of self-esteem. And this self-esteem cannot be based on solid accomplishments, dedication or some money in the bank. It must be based on *you* as a human being. You must learn to love and cherish yourself simply as a human being, giving yourself the same kind of respect and esteem that you would give a famous person or a good friend. The main lesson of cognitive therapy is to have self-esteem.

Now who, you ask, could possibly have any objection to *that*?

Mark me down as one having strong objections to it!

I have three basic criticisms of cognitive therapy.

A. Cognitive therapy delivers what in theology we call *cheap grace*. Cognitive therapy does this, moreover, by preaching a sermon! The therapist exhorts his patient to change his thinking habits—alone—all by himself. He alone can give himself self-esteem. "It's up to you," says the therapist.

Precisely because this grace is cheap rather than worthless, it will succeed in helping the patient just a little bit. By submitting to the authority and advice of the therapist, there will come a superficial, temporary benefit. Submission to *any* authority, even a chiropractor or a veterinarian, will produce some freedom from symptoms. But this is all we can look for. The help given is superficial and temporary.

B. Cognitive therapy encourages the "weak" person to grow into a strong person by exerting even more of his power than in the past.

The doctor encourages the patient to see himself as a weak person, struggling valiantly to become a strong human being. You recall the diagram on page 44 showing a person (outside the human race) who is struggling valiantly for a place in the human family. The doctor now adds his professional power to the powers of the patient in the hope that he will now become strong enough to "join the human race."

Freedom from depression, however, works the other way around. First we must become weak, powerless, played-out. Not only that! We have to resign as god. All the problems and trouble into which we get ourselves come from playing god.

C. Cognitive therapy ignores the Living God.

There simply is no lasting help for any of our human problems until we give Him a central place in their solution.

Exactly how can God become the healer of the troubled life of a depressed person?

First, the depressed person should be asked whether he wishes to fight on using his own power, or whether he is ready to surrender his life, his will and his power to Almighty God. The most a counselor can do in this situation is encourage the counselee to make it a clear-cut decision. The counselee's answer must be a clear, unequivocal *yes* or *no*.

Secondly, with God as the Highest Power of the depressed person, the problem of guilt needs to be addressed. Most depression is legitimately earned. There is invariably a need for confession. The wise counselor encourages the counselee to examine the relationships of his life and then, with assurances of confidentiality, to speak the unspeakable. There must follow then assurances of *God's* pardon, for no man can effectively deal with another man's guilt.

But there is more.

The counselor would then suggest carefully chosen *actions* which the counselee can take in his life situation. Perhaps there is need to offer an apology to someone, to pay a debt, or grant forgiveness.

Cognitive therapy says in effect that first you must get the right thoughts about yourself and then you will feel better. God says, *No, not that way. First surrender your life to Me, no matter how it feels.* First the *action.* The action of surrender, of restitution, requesting forgiveness, or loving the unloveable. And once you have *acted,* your thoughts will begin to change and, still later, your feelings. "Seek ye first the kingdom of God and his righteousness; and all these things shall be added unto you" (Matt. 6:33).

6. I, as a person, need help quite as much as any mental hospital patient.

The world of counseling proceeds on the assumption that we, the counselors, are the healthy ones and they, the counselees, are the ones who are sick. This is absurd. Such a delusion immediately disqualifies a person from being an effective helper. How can God's blessing rest upon a lie?

The first qualification of a human helper is that he must have settled, by a full surrender to God, the issue of power in his life. Until that is done, the counselor must base everything he says on his own egocentric viewpoint. It makes no difference how sincere and willing to help the counselor may be. He is sincerely wrong. His view of the world—namely, that he is ultimate—is a fantasy and he is forced to speak on the basis of his fantasy. The only way he can come into reality is to abandon his dead god and submit to the Living God.

But that is not enough.

A counselor must also have someone in his life who functions as *his* counselor on a continuing basis. There is a good reason for this.

Counselors, without even realizing it, can easily drift into an attitude of omniscience. This is the blind spot, particularly of educated people. A little education, a few academic degrees, have a bewitching way of assuring the counselor that he knows what he is doing and where he is going with the counselee.

Such an attitude is often fatal for both parties. It happens because the counselor is himself deluded. He says, "I am OK, but you are not OK."

Centuries ago, the Roman Caesars, returning from their foreign conquests, rode in great glory in their victory parades. All of Rome turned out to see their leader followed by the vanquished captives and the spoils of war being paraded through the streets. There was always one of Caesar's servants riding with him in the parade whose task it was to repeatedly whisper these words into his ear: "Enjoy thy fame, O Caesar, but thou too art mortal, as mortal as those thou hast slain."

Wise counselors always ask someone to whisper in their ear, "You, too, must be helped—indeed, *especially* you, for you are constantly in danger of speaking out of a deluded mind."

7

Power in the Minister and the Medic

I propose in this chapter to show how our deep power urges are expressed through the pastoral and the psychiatric professions. The only reason I limit myself to these two professions is simply because I have a fairly intimate knowledge of each.

Looking back on my life, I know now how God led me into the ministry. When only a young boy, God dazzled me with the power of an old Dutch Dominee*. My Father knew the Dominee well. He loved to tell the story of how Dominee helped Bessie to overcome her fear of having committed the unpardonable sin.

Every time Dominee visited Bessie, she would tearfully complain that she had committed the unpardonable sin mentioned in the Scriptures. Her pastor would then patiently explain to her that she had misinterpreted the Bible, that people who commit that sin could not care less, that she was a Christian to whom God had given a total forgiveness.

It made no difference. Bessie *knew* she had committed the unpardonable sin. And Dominee knew she had not. Year after year the faithful pastor visited his guilt-ridden sheep. Dominee patiently tried everything—prayer, books to read, pleading, scolding, tears.

And then, one day, the Dominee's patience finally ran out.

---

* In the Reformed tradition, the clergy were often given this title.

POWER GREATER THAN OURSELVES

Bessie had been going on for half an hour about what a hopeless sinner she was and how she wished she had never committed that unpardonable sin. Suddenly, the Dominee jumped to his feet, knocking over his chair. He strode decisively over to Bessie and confronted her squarely.

"I am sick and tired, Bessie, of your endless complaining about the unpardonable sin. It's going to stop—today!"

And with that, Dominee grabbed Bessie by the arm and pulled her down to her knees in prayer.

"Now you repeat after me!" yelled the kneeling parson. "Lord!"

"Lord," whispered the startled Bessie.

"This has got to stop!"

"This has got to stop." Bessie's voice was very weak.

"I've confessed the unpardonable sin for the last time!"

Softly: "I've confessed the unpardonable sin for the last time."

"Louder, Bessie!"

"Louder, Bessie."

"And this has got to stop!"

"And this has got to stop."

"Thank You, Lord."

"Thank You, Lord."

"Amen."

"Amen."

Dominee made a quick exit while Bessie was still on her knees.

According to my father who told me this story, Bessie never again complained about her sinful depravity. The guilt had left her from the day that the courageous Dominee pulled Bessie to her knees. Indeed, thereafter, she was a really changed woman.

I was ten years old when Father told me about Bessie and Dominee. I remember well my reaction. I said, "Wow! What a Dominee!" I was deeply impressed with the boldness, the decisiveness and the *power* of Dominee. Just look at what he had done with Bessie!

I began to figure that if Dominee could do *that* with people, becoming a dominee was for me. Though I was unable to get it into words at the time, I sensed that a dominee had *power.*

Power in the Minister and the Medic

As I now reflect on my thirty years in the ministry, it is clear to me that it is primarily a lust for power which drives most of us into that sacred office. Such an ignoble motivation must naturally be concealed. Some will surely deny it. Perhaps, in many cases, the pastor may even be quite unaware of such a motive. But there is little doubt but that the ministry draws those who are power-oriented. Just look at some of the ways in which the Christian ministry offers opportunities to those bent on acquiring power.

1. A minister claims a divine call to do his work. I happen to believe that *everyone* has a divine call to do his work. The only difference between the minister's call and a layman's call is simply that the minister, perhaps unconsciously, *stresses* the divine origin of his call. This appeal to the divine is thought to add power to his call. But it really does not. Simply saying it does not make it true. It is all in the pastor's head. True, his call is of God. But so is everyone else's. Most pastors, however, think their calling is more special.

2. Ordination to ministerial office registers with many as a new tool to acquire power. The use of exalting titles—reverend, father, pastor—tends to give the man of God that elevated position which his hunger for power needs. With a title before his name and a few degrees following it, a preacher inevitably feels a sense of accomplishment and a worthiness to wield power.

Perhaps this also explains why so many women are seeking ordination. Surely it is not because there is such a crying need for pastors; most denominations have more pastors than they can use. The eagerness of females for ordination, however, is easily explained by the influence of modern feminism which seeks to give more power to women.

3. A minister, when he accepts a call to a typical congregation, usually walks into:

    a. A warm reception he has done nothing to merit.

    b. A congregation of people he did not assemble.

    c. A pulpit he did not establish.

    d. A church building he did not build.

    e. The love of a people to whom he has as yet not given anything.

Such an experience is enough to intoxicate even the dullest of God's saints. Such drunkenness can be the occasion for self-elevation, conceit and imperialistic fantasies. It happens.

4. The new pastor of a church is immediately given the position of president of the governing body. The pastor does not have to patiently work his way up to such a position, nor does he have to eliminate other contenders. He is simply appointed the leader and immediately given the power of his office.

5. A pastor—even a newly-arrived pastor—is immediately empowered to deal with the most intimate and delicate issues among his parishioners. The pastor, sometimes quite untested, is asked for counsel regarding some of the thorniest problems in human life—marital conflicts, sexual problems, troubles between parents and their children, in-law rivalry, occupational problems—and the weightiest of all issues, spiritual problems. A pastor is immediately trusted by his congregation to be a reliable guide to his congregation with all that this implies.

Most of us were immediately staggered by all these expectations. But as we began to cope with the work, every sincere pastor was at least aware he might exploit the work to enhance his own personal power.

6. Notice also how the pastor of a church is given authority to teach the congregation. Week after week, people will listen to him preach and take seriously what he says. Changes will take place in their lives as a result of their pastor's ministry. Each congregation, with shocking trustfulness, entrusts their pastor with this extremely influential power to preach and teach.

7. In most churches, a pastor is given power to determine who may, and who may not use the church facilities. A close ministerial friend of mine denied the use of the sanctuary for the marriage of a young lady in the congregation. She had insisted that she and her fiance write their own marriage service, a common practice today. This very determined young woman then went out and found another pastor who was happy to allow them to write their own ceremony and marry them in her church. But the installed pastor saw what was happening and called a halt to her plans. Here is

another demonstration of pastoral power, in this case, it seems to me, rightly used.

8. A pastor is a power in the community. City officials immediately listen to the local pastor simply because he is the pastor. Policemen, I find, are quick to cooperate with a pastor, not because he is worthy of cooperation, but because of his office. That office gives the pastor power with people.

9. Finally, most pastors wield varying amounts of power through their membership on denominational boards and committees. A few especially ambitious and competitive individuals secure positions as denominational executives. The race is always hot for these positions, the more so because pastors, as a group, tend to be highly competitive. Pastors, it cannot be denied, love power.

Question: What is wrong with getting and using power?

Answer: Anyone who gets and uses power is doomed to squander it on himself unless he has come to terms with the Highest Power.

To get right to the point, the only qualified candidate for any position of power, is one who has surrendered to, and is currently submitted to, Divine Power. Until the issue of power is decisively settled in favor of God, a human being has no alternative but to play god. An unsurrendered person is doomed to the futile effort of seeking to be ultimate in his own crazy little world. To do this, he must step on some people, eliminate others, push, shove and work like a maniac (which he is) until he gains primacy.

There is plenty wrong with that.

I repeat, the person in whose life the issue of power has been settled in favor of God is alone qualified to handle power. That person will be marked by two major characteristics:

(1) He will wait to be sought out for an office; he will not seek it. Those who *must* have an office—any office—have already disqualified themselves as worthy candidates. The office seeker who bases his effort upon his lust for power has already disqualified himself.

POWER GREATER THAN OURSELVES

Candidates for office should ideally be *asked* to serve, rather than *seek* to serve.[1]

Granted, it seldom works that way. Even the God-oriented person is usually not *that* selfless. Certainly few pastors enter the ministry without actively seeking such a position. Look also at the political world and the business world. There the ambitious actively seek positions of power and authority. Even there, however, it is best if a person is selected and asked to serve. If one seeks office, it is often a real question whose needs he wants to serve—his own or others?

I must quickly add, however, that there is hope for even the most power-hungry individual if only he will, after securing his position of power, truly seek to serve. This brings me to the second characteristic of a person firmly under God's authority.

(2) He will seek a servant role.

Our Lord spelled this out with great clarity.

Two of the disciples, James and John, wanted power. Their mamma also wanted them to have power, so she went to Jesus and asked if her boys could each sit at his side when he became king. Jesus gently declined the offer of this power-hungry family.

The other ten disciples, however, were highly indignant at the two brothers. The ten wanted the power-pie cut in twelve, not two, equal pieces!

Jesus saw that it was time to address the problem of power. This is what He said: "You know that the rulers of the Gentiles lord it over them, and their great men exercise authority over them. It shall not be so among you; but whoever would be great among you must be your servant, and whoever would be first among you must be your slave" (Matt. 20:25-27).

At the Last Supper, Jesus again taught the lesson of servanthood by his own example. He wrapped a towel around himself, drew water and began to wash the disciple's feet. He who was the Highest Power

---

[1] In medieval times, one of the requirements for becoming a bishop was that one should *not* want to be one. The candidate was asked: "Do you want to be a bishop?" He was expected to answer: "Nolo episcopan." ("I do not want to be a bishop.") (Editor's note)

condescended to wash their feet. "If I then, your Lord and Teacher, have washed your feet, you also ought to wash one another's feet. For I have given you an example, that you also should do as I have done to you."

Only that pastor who is a true and faithful servant of God and His people is qualified to rightly handle the power of his office.

When it comes to having power over people in today's society, a pastor is a small-time operator compared to a psychiatrist. A hundred years ago it was far differen.. Today, however, the undisputed power potentates are psychiatrists. Only the federal government has more power over people. Consider:

A psychiatrist assumes complete control over the life of his patient. This ambitious assignment is accomplished partly by means of verbal therapy and, more forcibly, by drugs and shock treatments. The doctor never entertains a doubt that he can manipulate and change the patient's feelings for the better. In cases where the treatment is a failure and the patient gets worse, the blame is never assigned to the psychiatrist. The fault always lies with the uncooperative patient's stubborn chemistry or bad attitude.

The psychiatrist, therefore, not only has complete power over his patient but also the power never to fail in his treatment. This, as far as power is concerned, is the best of all possible worlds! But there is more.

In our society, a psychiatrist has power to label a person as mentally ill and then keep him permanently incarcerated in a mental hospital. In order to qualify for this kind of treatment, a person must either exhibit some social behavior which is somewhat odd, or make funny noises for no reason, or say a few sentences which make no sense, or express a few shocking fantasies, or even threaten another person. If our candidate really wants to live dangerously, he must tell the psychiatrist that "someone is really out to get me." This is usually a sure ticket to a mental hospital because that is paranoid thinking of the kind which points towards schizophrenia.

There have been a number of scientific experiments made by perfectly normal people who faked their symptoms and easily gained entrance as patients to a mental hospital. Because most psychiatrists believe they cannot be fooled, it was no problem at all to be admitted. There are other cases, however, where the psychiatrist knows that a person is *not* mentally ill, but the psychiatrist will nonetheless commit him to a mental hospital. This happens when a mentally-healthy criminal pleads not guilty by reason of insanity. If a psychiatrist can be found to establish this criminal's "insanity," the doors of the mental hospital will swing open to the "criminal." Psychiatric power is impressive to watch.

Once one gains entrance to a mental hospital as a bona fide patient, he can be forced to take drugs and undergo electro-shock treatments. I have witnessed more than one patient fleeing from the ward at the news that the psychiatrist was soon to arrive with his "little box" (the electro-shock machine). Most patients were terrorized by it. The patient, at least in state mental hospitals, has no choice. The mental patient gets "zapped" because of a decision made solely by the psychiatrist.

When this mental patient begins to recover his senses, he usually becomes a new kind of problem. As he feels better and continues to recover, he becomes a discipline problem on the ward. In extreme cases, because of his improved health, he may want so badly to be discharged that he will tongue-lash, or even assault, an attendant. The psychiatrist is ready for such a contingency. The "sick" person is overpowered and placed in a seclusion room. Theoretically, the uncooperative person can be indefinitely confined in a mental hospital. A psychiatrist has power to do that.

These displays of psychiatric power are indeed impressive but I have waited until now to really make the point. There is the case of a woman who went to a psychiatrist for some help with her troubled life. He found her to be depressed, particularly by the burden of her job and housework. One of her complaints was that she had a very poor washing machine and was falling behind in washing her clothes.

Could the good doctor do anything to help her? Indeed he could! He was prepared to get her a brand-new washing machine!

On what basis? Her emotional stability demanded it.

Who would pay for it? Good old Uncle Sam.

Power in the Minister and the Medic

Can a psychiatrist really do that? All it requires is that he write a prescription for a washing machine.

Perhaps you may never make use of psychiatric power to buy your wife a new washing machine, but there may yet come a day when you will feel the awesome power of a psychiatrist in your life.

Imagine yourself on your deathbed. Medical science has done its best to get a little more mileage out of you but now only machines are keeping you alive. Fortunately, you are still conscious. You are a believer and have no fear of meeting your Maker and Redeemer. You have conferred with your close family and have come to a difficult decision: the machines are to be turned off.

But not so fast!

No one can touch the machines before a psychiatrist has been summoned to check you over. After all, you may be hallucinating. The machines will keep running until the psychiatrist has examined you and determined that you are rational.

After that, you are allowed to go meet your Lord. Finally.

While your soul is resting in peace with the Lord, however, your psychiatrist may still not be finished with you. He may have very much to say about that last will and testament you have left behind.

Let us imagine that you have left behind some very greedy adult children who are most unhappy upon reading your will. It turns out that you generously gave ninety percent of your wealth to the church and charitable causes. Can anything be done to help these poor orphaned children?

Yes, of course.

They must go out and find what is called a forensic psychiatrist. They are not cheap, but he just may be able to find a way to bring comfort to those grieving children.

If the psychiatrist, on the basis of "solid" information supplied by children and friends, can establish that the deceased was really not very rational at the time he made out his will, it may be possible for the judge to set that horrible will aside—and give the money to the grieving children!

Such is the power of modern psychiatry.

POWER GREATER THAN OURSELVES

I believe that pastors and psychiatrists—indeed, all professional people—are lured into their respective professions primarily by a greed for power. Granted that we may be unaware of this when we choose a profession, but it is *there* nonetheless, deep in our hearts. Power is the universal prime motivator of the human heart. If that heart is egocentrically positioned, the power amassed will corrupt the person and inflict great damage on people affected by it.

If, by the grace of God, egocentric power dies and is replaced by God, the Highest Power, there is then hope that good may come to many people.

A friend of mine, on reading the rough draft of this chapter, asked if I could somehow find something positive to say about the work done by psychiatrists.

I am happy to oblige my friend.

Yes, I do have something good to say about the good work done not only by psychiatrists but also pastors.

First, pastors. We have an example close at hand—Dominee and Bessie. How do we account for the dramatic help given to Bessie, this woman who was obsessed with the thought that she had committed the unpardonable sin?

We must first understand that Bessie, through the years, had become her own highest power. All the egocentric strivings of childhood were still in her, working hard to establish her in her world as the highest power, the *queen.* Look how she opposed Dominee for years on this problem of the unpardonable sin! Every time it was discussed Bessie always came out the *winner,* a winner who not only loved all the sympathy and attention she was receiving, but one with a unique unsolvable problem. That is quite a winner.

Dominee banged his head against this problem until he could stand it no longer. In a moment of holy boldness, he decided to use his power against Bessie's power. He would *force* Bessie to back down from her position and accept his solution to her suffering. With that, he pulled Bessie to her knees, gave her words to say in prayer, and told her he wanted to hear no more of her nonsense.

It was a dangerous, critical moment. Bessie's resistance could have hardened. She could have given the Dominee a kick in the shins and told him to get out and never come back. Had she done that, she would have remained her own ultimate authority, her own highest power.

But Bessie, undoubtedly because of her undeniable suffering and extreme fatigue, decided that she was at the end of her self-rule. She would surrender her failing power to a higher power, in this case God, as represented in Dominee. She agreed to let go of her understanding of herself and submit to Dominee's. Bessie was no longer ultimate. She agreed to be Number Two.

And suddenly, the miracle occurred! All the worry, struggle, fear and self-pity were suddenly gone. Bessie was free! And she knew it!

The theological explanation for this miracle in Bessie's life is embarrassingly simple. Any person who maintains his egocentric position in the world lives a lie. He makes himself the victim of a lie because he *is* a living lie. He embraces the lie that he is god, that he is the ultimate one. All the suffering connected with this grandest of all delusions is earned suffering.

The moment this god-player voluntarily leaves his delusion that he is Number One and becomes a human being, his egocentric power dies. He may then submit to the power and authority of God. This automatically and dramatically frees him from the distress and pain which his sin has brought upon him.

Incidentally, Dominee also found freedom in this episode from the tyranny of himself. It was only when Dominee had nothing more to say to Bessie that he went to God with her. Dominee did this as a defeated, failing pastor. Once he could confess that, God could use him to help Bessie.

Let me summarize what we have learned in one sentence:

> Those who are in control
> go out of control
> until they come under Control.

This is the master key to life.

And now a few words about the work done by psychiatrists and psychologists.

POWER GREATER THAN OURSELVES

There are now in the U.S. around fifty-five thousand psychiatrists and psychologists who treat approximately thirty-four million people at a cost of about thirteen billion dollars a year for treatment.

Psychiatrists and psychologists have grouped themselves into more than 250 different kinds of therapy. To confuse the picture even more, most therapists are eclectic. They freely borrow from one another and from the different schools of psychotherapy.

For years now, research has been going on to determine just how much people are being helped by the various approaches. Researchers find that no matter what brand of psychotherapy they investigate, they usually find that from sixty to eighty percent of the buyers are helped to some degree, usually for a short time. This is surprising in view of the fact that the different kinds of psychotherapy are radically different from one another. Freudians have nothing to do with the behaviorists. The Jungians do something quite different from the Rogerians. These schools differ from each other as much as medical doctors from veterinarians and chiropractors from dentists.

The question remains. Why does everyone receive some temporary benefit, no matter who the benefactor is?

The answer is simple.

Those who place themselves under a higher authority—even if the authority be satanic—will receive some temporary benefit. They will feel better. Generally, they will improve somewhat. They will be a bit freer of their symptoms for a time.

You remember the power of a placebo. If you *believe,* no matter what concoction you imbibe, it will help you. Placebos work so well simply because the patient voluntarily places himself under a higher authority.

It is the same in counseling. You select a counselor. At first you approach him cautiously. He talks. You talk. And then, at some point in the conversation, you surrender the control of yourself to the counselor. You become, in that moment, a believer.

What that means, however, is that you are no longer in control of yourself. You have thrown the controls over to your newly-chosen higher power—the counselor.

Now that's all right if your counselor correctly uses his authority and takes you to God. But if your counselor keeps you in his hands and under his own power, a terrible tragedy will befall you. You will have suffered all for nothing! All the pain and distress you endured were fruitless and now you will be hurled back into your crazy, egocentric world to suffer all over again. Such is fate of one who remains his own highest power.

So if you go to a psychiatrist or a psychologist, make sure you get one in whom the problem of power has been settled. By that I mean that the counselor must be a person who is secondary to the Highest Power, God. The counselor, to be of any help to you, must encourage you to (1) surrender to God and (2) obey Him in specific actions suggested by the counselor.

Entrust yourself, therefore, only to that person who truly knows and trusts in God sufficiently to take you in self-surrender to Him. If your psychiatrist or psychologist carries such credentials, he will be a great blessing to you.

8

Power in Sports

In our study of the phenomenon of power, we must take a brief look at sports. I am convinced that sport is the channel through which flows some of our deepest religious yearnings.

I say that because even in ancient Greece, athletics were always combined with religious festivals. Each Greek city in the Fourth Century B.C. had its own stadium in which the images of a dozen gods and goddesses were paraded prior to the games. The spectators worshipped these deities, yes, but also earnestly invoked them to grant victory to the contestants they had selected to win. By the time the pageantry was over and the games begun, the spectators were identified with their favorite athletes. Gambling brought the spectators to a point of complete involvement with the game and the contestants.

While the Greeks went more for sports—wrestling, boxing, the pankration, running, pentathlon, jumping, javelin-throwing, discus— the Romans had a taste for gladiatorial combat and especially, chariot-racing. As with the Greeks, the Romans began their sporting events with religious ceremonies. The gods were invoked by the participants and the demons invoked to curse their opponents. Gambling was much heavier among the Romans than the Greeks.

What are we to make of this strange mixture of idolatry and gambling in the ancient world of sports?

Both seem to me explainable simply as efforts to achieve power. Why did these people worship idols? To gain power. Idol images were regarded as the dwelling place of supernatural beings. If you honored the image, you pleased the god whose power was resident in that image. A pleased god was able and willing to help your favorite athlete win his race.

Greater participation in the athlete's victory could be accomplished by gambling on the event. Here again the god was needed. The gods were supposed to have the power to make winners.

What is this strange thing called *competition* which is at the very core of every sport? Why must we always determine who is the winner? Why should winning be so important to us?

In answer to these questions, we should recognize that not all games and sports feed on the competitive spirit. There is such a thing as engaging in a sport or playing a game in such a way that winning or losing is an indifferent matter.

When I play a game of chess with my wife, for example, I do so to relax, divert my mind and simply be involved with the woman I love. It is play for both of us. We are refreshed by it. Who wins or loses is an indifferent matter. It really does not matter—very much.

For I have a confession to make. I must admit that even in this relaxed game of chess, I prefer to win. Winning gives me a slight, momentary joy which losing does not give. I must admit, too, that if my wife consistently defeated me in chess, I would soon give up the game in favor of something in which I would have some hope of occasionally winning.

Now my question is this: How do we account for this universal need to win? Why could we not all simply agree to do our best and let it go at that? No. We must win over others. Even in simple parlor games, we strain for victory. The entire sports and gambling world is dedicated to this one goal of separating the winners from the losers. Just look at the scope of this frantic, frenzied, world-wide search to find the victors.

Look at this list of modern sports: archery, auto-racing, badminton, baseball, basketball, bicycle-racing, billiards, bobsledding, bowling, bowls, boxing, Bridge, canoeing, chess, cricket, curling, cycling, dog-racing, fencing, fishing, football, golf, gymnastics, Highland Games, hockey, horse-racing, hunting, ice hockey, ice skating, judo, tennis, modern pentathlon, motor-boating, parachute jumping, pigeon-racing, polo, roller-skating, rowing, shooting, show jumping, skiing, squash rackets, swimming, table tennis, tobogganing, track and field sports, trampoline, volley-ball, water skiing, weight-lifting, wrestling, yachting.

At this very moment, hundreds of thousands of people are pressing themselves to the limits of human endurance to excel in these sports. And millions more are interested spectators and dedicated fans who are completely swept up in the spirit of this search to find the winners.

Again I ask, why? What is so important about determining who is the better boxer? Why are we so interested in determining who is the world's best pingpong player? What difference does it make who wins the World Series? Why are all these sports enthusiasts urging their favorite champions on to new victories?

There is a beautifully simple theological answer to these difficult questions.

This universal competitive urge in man is a sure sign that he is (1) trying to be god and (2) seeking the true God.

The competitive spirit in man is a natural fruit of his innate egocentrism. Each human being is born with a flourishing self-centeredness. The young, again, are completely self-concerned and, in this sense, very god-like—as they should be at that stage.

These deep, strong egocentric tendencies, however, thrust us into a senseless competition with other egocentrics. The race to be a god—Number One—is begun in early childhood and can continue even to our deathbeds. Not knowing God, we are doomed to play god.

The competitive urge, however, is also a sure sign that we are in search of the true, Living God. In the sports contest—whatever kind of competition it may be—we acknowledge that there is a person, a power greater than all others. We symbolically admit thereby that there is an Ultimate One who excels all other powers. Just as our egocentrism points to the need for God at the center of our lives, so do sports point to the place in our lives which God is intended to fill. We gamesters and sports enthusiasts, yes, even we gamblers, are constantly in search of the Perfect Winner. As surfers search for the Perfect Wave (but never find it), so we search for Number One.

But He is not one of us.

He is God.

In the most profound sense, Christianity asserts that all games are finished! They are played out! All the passion, pain and sometimes even death that went into these games, is finished. And idolatry—both ancient and modern—is played out. The Winner has been decisively determined. He is the living, supernatural Lord of us all!

The alternative to such a theological understanding of sports is to see sports as a modern example of the so-called evolutionary process. In this view, man, who is the most highly developed animal, preserves his species exactly as all the other animals do—by eliminating the weak, thereby insuring "the survival of the fittest." Early in history, these contests of power were worked out between individuals, families and clans. In more modern times, contests of power have been decided on the level of nations which periodically go to war with each other. Since the dawn of recorded history, it is estimated that one person out of four has been killed in such wars. Is it any wonder, asks the secularist, that we seek an alternative to this vicious process which evolution thrusts upon us? The best alternative, we are told, to this cruel evolution at work in our species, is sport. From an evolutionary point of view, sports are laudable because they serve to sublimate our instinct for war and rebellion.

The basic assumption of the evolutionary position is that power is intrinsic to man. Whatever power there is, comes from within himself. Christians immediately sense the error of this position, knowing that Power (God) is extrinsic to man. And further, we understand that we must come to terms with this Omnipotent Other, once and for all settling this nagging issue of power. It does not interest us to determine who among us has most power. The issue is not between man and man. The issue is between man and God.

Power in Sports

On that happy day when the power issue is finally and decisively resolved in favor of the Lord, we are ready to play games the way they should be played—for fun, relaxation and exercise. No longer need we use sports to achieve a pretended divinity. Nor will we worship those who have established themselves as sports idols.

9

Power Among the Nations

The ideas for this chapter began to form in my mind on an unforgettable day in 1944. I was in France, sitting in the turret of a Sherman tank, feeding bullets into a machine gun.

My tank commander suddenly gave the command to cease fire. Looking through my periscope, I strained to see what was happening. When the noise had quieted and the dust settled, it became apparent that a small part of World War II was ending—at least for five Germans. They wanted to surrender.

The first things to be thrown out of their trench were five rifles and two small anti-tank weapons. I saw next a piece of white cloth on a stick raised high for us to see. Thirty seconds later, a helmet was slowly raised on another stick. This was a test for our reaction to their surrender. Finally, the five men slowly emerged from the trench with their hands up. I was able to see the fear and terror in their eyes as they walked towards our tank.

I next remember hearing the voice of my tank commander on the intercom radio. "Traverse left, turret machine gun. Five enemy infantry. Open fire!"

I could not believe it!

I knew my tank commander was a rough-and-tumble regular army man who had trained all his life for battle, but I was not prepared to shoot men in cold blood.

"Repeat the order!" I shouted incredulously.

"Five krauts at eleven o'clock. Open fire, gunner."

POWER GREATER THAN OURSELVES

Now I was not the gunner. I was the loader of the gun and, unfortunately for those Germans, only a corporal. Corporals may not wield much power in a tank, but one thing we do have is control of the ammunition. So, using the only power I had, I twisted the machine-belt and jammed the weapon. As I leisurely repaired the machine-gun, the crisis passed. My tank commander angrily threatened me with a court-martial, but his threat was empty.

I was badly shaken by the entire incident, though not because of the threatened court martial. What upset me so deeply was a suddenly realization that *the entire war was wrong*. The morality at work in my tank was just as rotten as anything in the German army. I suddenly realized that it was wrong, wrong, wrong for all of us to be there shooting at each other.

I remember trying to talk myself into a good reason for continuing to fight the Germans. Did not Hitler need to be stopped? Was not the entire free world pitted against that raging political monster called fascism?

I could answer such questions affirmatively, but I now had nothing but distress and distaste for the means (armed warfare) of accomplishing these good goals. Almost reluctantly, I realized I was becoming a pacifist. A few weeks later, the brutal death of my tank-commander took away any resistance still in me. My commanding officer knew it, and threw me into a tank-mechanic position where I would not contaminate the fighting spirit of the entire company.

I laid aside the entire issue of war and pacifism for the next fifteen years. The Korean and Vietnam Wars did not affect me at all except as a taxpayer. There was no particular need to come to a decision on these matters. I was busy doing other things.

All this was changed when my ministry turned in the direction of pastoral counseling. I was again faced with the violence/non-violence issue as I addressed myself to the mini-wars of inter-personal and marital relationships. Later in this chapter, I will explain how non-violence had a direct bearing on counseling. First, however, it would be helpful to look at the basic New Testament passages which bear on the violence/non-violence issue.

Our Lord, in the Sermon on the Mount, clearly laid down the divine principles of non-violence.

> You have heard that it was said, "An eye for an eye and a tooth for a tooth." But I say to you, Do not resist one who is evil. But if any one strikes you on the right cheek, turn to him the other also; and if any one would sue you and take your coat, let him have your cloak as well; and if any one forces you to go one mile, go with him two miles. Give to him who begs from you, and do not refuse him who would borrow from you. You have heard that it was said, "You shall love your neighbor and hate your enemy." But I say to you, Love your enemies and pray for those who persecute you, so that you may be sons of your Father who is in heaven. (Matt. 5:38-45)

> So whatever you wish that men would do to you, do so to them; for this is the law and the prophets. (Matt. 7:12)

These words were perfectly applied to the reality of the crucifixion event. Our Lord's first words from the cross—"Father, forgive them; for they know not what they do" (Luke 23:34)—was an exact application of His teaching on non-violence.

Turning to the Apostle Paul, we sense his profound grasp of the teaching of our Lord in Romans 12:14-21:

> Bless those who persecute you; bless and do not curse them. Rejoice with those who rejoice, weep with those who weep. Live in harmony with one another; do not be haughty, but associate with the lowly; never be conceited. Repay no one evil for evil, but take thought for what is noble in the sight of all. If possible, so far as it depends upon you, live

peaceably with all. Beloved, never avenge your-selves, but leave it to the wrath of God; for it is written, "Vengeance is mine, I will repay, says the Lord." No, "if your enemy is hungry, feed him; if he is thirsty, give him drink; for by so doing you will heap burning coals upon his head." Do not be overcome by evil, but overcome evil with good.

As with our Lord, Paul practiced the teaching of non-violence in the work of preaching the Gospel. "When reviled, we bless; when persecuted, we endure; when slandered, we try to conciliate; we have become, and are now, as the refuse of the world, the offscouring of all things" (1 Cor. 4:12-13).

Peter—that man of violence in the Garden of Gethsemane—was told to "put your sword back into its place; for all who take the sword will perish by the sword" (Matt. 26:52). After Pentecost, Peter was inspired to exalt in the non-violence of Christ, "leaving you an example, that you should follow in his steps. He committed no sin; no guile was found on his lips. When he was reviled, he did not revile in return; when he suffered, he did not threaten; but he trusted in him who judges justly" (1 Pet. 2:21-23).

The basic point made by these New Testament passages is that we cannot seriously love our neighbor while aiming a gun at him. Jesus made no exceptions to the universal command to "love your enemies." Many of those whom we count our enemies, are those Christ came to save. Since He is the savior of the world, we are commanded not only to turn the other cheek, but to actively, aggressively love our so-called enemies.

Those who speak of a "just" war have, it seems to me, missed our Lord's point. I suppose most Americans would argue that our cause was just in the war with Japan during 1941-1945. After all, we were attacked at Pearl Harbor. I, too, would agree that our cause was just. But I no longer feel that our *response* to the injustice was correct. Further, I would want to argue that December 7, 1941, was not the time to insist upon justice, but rather a time to actively love the "enemy" and do him good.

Power Among the Nations

Our innate egocentrism (individually and nationally) causes us to quickly respond to evil with a threat of judgment rather than an invasion of love. Such is not the message of our Lord. If I understand His message, love takes precedence over every other virtue. Love is greater than justice. So far as justice is concerned, we are not called to bring our enemies, but ourselves, to justice. We must leave our enemies to the judgment of the Just Judge of all the earth.

At the time of Pearl Harbor we Americans fell into the error of placing the issue of justice above the issue of love. Millions of people die when we rush in with justice rather than love.

How could we have concretely loved the Japanese on December 7, 1941? We could have used restraint and patience. More importantly and more realistically, in the decade prior to 1941, America could have persistently and creatively done Japan good, as we certainly have in the post-war years. Look how we have respected and assisted post-war Japan! It is the same with West Germany. Indeed, we now count them our good friends and we want them to be strong nations. Now we love them, having first brought them to justice. Had we loved them first, there would have been less need for justice and millions of lives would have been spared.

"Make love your aim" (1 Cor. 14:1) because love is greater than justice. Our mistake is that we rush in with justice when we should rush in with love.

Can we realistically expect any modern state to act non-violently? Yes. William Robert Miller, in his book *Nonviolence* (Association Press, NY 1964) cites a number of interesting examples of nations which have effectively used the "weapon" of non-violence. In the years 1859-1867, the Hungarian people secured their political rights in a bloodless, non-violent struggle with their Austrian oppressors. At the turn of the century, Finland resisted the Tsar of Russia with a complete general strike which shut down the entire nation, securing for a time the political rights upon which the Finns insisted. It is true that the victory was of short duration and the Finns lapsed back into violence, but there is no denying that for a time, there, non-violence worked. The Danes and Norwegians effectively resisted the Nazi army of occupation between 1940-1943. And finally, there are the shining examples of non-violence in India and Ghana during the post-war period. There is no question but that modern nations can adopt non-violent principles and prevail in their struggles with oppressor states.

God's love, working through non-violent agents, has been strikingly demonstrated to us in the lives of three modern men— Dietrich Bonhoeffer, Mohandas K. Gandhi and Martin Luther King, Jr. I would like to quote each man briefly on the subject of non-violence.

It was Bonhoeffer who wrote:

> The only way to overcome evil is to let it run itself to a standstill because it does not find the resistance it is looking for. Resistance merely creates further evil and adds fuel to the flames. But when evil meets no opposition and encounters no obstacle but only patient endurance, its sting is drawn, and at last it meets an opponent which is more than its match. Of course this can only happen when the last ounce of resistance is abandoned, and the renunciation of revenge is complete. Then evil cannot find its mark, it can breed no further evil, and is left barren.
>
> The Cost of Discipleship by Dietrich Bonhoeffer
> Pages 157-158
> Macmillan Co., NY

Gandhi had this to say:

> . . . Suffering in one's own person is . . . the essence of non-violence and is the chosen substitute for violence to others. It is not because I value life low that I can countenance with joy thousands voluntarily losing their lives for Satyagraha (voluntary sacrifice), but because I know that it results in the long run in the least loss of life, and what is more, it ennobles those who lose their lives . . . .
> (Unless) Europe is to commit suicide, some nation

will have to dare to disarm herself and take large risks. The level of non-violence in that nation . . . will naturally have risen so high as to command universal respect. Her judgments will be unerring, her decisions will be firm, her capacity for heroic self-sacrifice will be great, and she will want to live as much for other nations as for herself . . . . (from *Young India,* October 8, 1925)

Finally, listen to Martin Luther King, Jr.:

How do we love our enemies? First, we must develop and maintain the capacity to forgive. He who is devoid of the power to forgive is devoid of the power to love. It is impossible even to begin the act of loving one's enemies without the prior acceptance of the necessity, over and over again, of forgiving those who inflict evil and injury upon us. It is also necessary to realize that the forgiving act must always be initiated by the person who has been wronged, the victim of some great hurt, the recipient of some tortuous injustice, the absorber of some terrible act of oppression. The wrongdoer may request forgiveness. He may come to himself, and, like the prodigal son, move up some dusty road, his heart palpitating with the desire for forgiveness. But only the injured neighbor, the loving father back home, can really pour out the warm waters of forgiveness.

Strength to Love by Martin Luther King, Jr.
Page 35
Harper and Row, NY 1963

None of us need wait until a new world war is upon us to practice non-violence. It cries out to be practiced in our inter-personal relationships. We see the ultimate test of our non-violent love in the intimacy of troubled marital relationships. I want now to present a severely troubled marriage to which the basic principles of non-violence were effectively applied through counseling. The following example illustrates the handling of verbal violence on the part of a husband against his wife.

The marriage between Fred and Maggie had always been difficult. But now, after fifteen years, the relationship was moving into more frequent verbal violence. Fred was usually the aggressor. He could use his tongue like a knife. Still, Maggie refused to be intimidated. On several occasions they traded blows. To make matters worse, Fred was doing some serious drinking. Since Fred was in no mood to talk to a pastoral counselor, Maggie came alone to my study. She wanted to know what she was doing wrong in the marriage.

So I told her. I told her she must never again be drawn into a slugfest with her husband, no matter how angry she was with him. Nothing could ever justify it. She was not to fight him physically even if he drunkenly provoked it. If Fred tried to start a fight while under the influence of liquor, Maggie was to flee from the home until he sobered up.

That still left the problem of what to do when Fred and Maggie would get into a fight when no liquor was involved. In such cases, I devised a non-violent strategy which, at some length, I explained to Maggie.

Her first response to her angry husband must be one of self-examination leading to an apology on her part. Maggie listened, but really had no idea of what I was saying until I turned to an example from her own life.

"Do you remember the fight you and Fred had over the food money at home? He was angry with you for over-spending your food budget and neglecting to take advantage of the food sales. This terrible argument escalated into an exchange of blows, you recall.

"You responded to Fred, at the time, with an attack on him. He was unfair. He did not understand. He was making a big issue out of nothing. And he was a bully to hit you the way he did.

"What I am now suggesting, Maggie, is an entirely new approach. The attack on Fred must be abandoned. You must look at yourself and your own faults. You know very well that Fred is right in some ways. You *do* over-spend and over-buy. You have admitted to me that you must frequently throw food away because your refrigerator is so full. And we have also talked about your careless attitude with money.

"If you really want to *do* something about your marriage, Maggie, you must get honest with yourself, admit your faults to Fred and then ask his forgiveness."

Maggie and I then did some role playing. I played the part of an angry, upset Fred. It took some time for the lesson to register with Maggie, but her sense of desperation assisted her. She was learning to do two things in response to Fred: (1) to look within herself first and (2) to apologize for any faults and weaknesses in herself.

Having well mastered the first step of non-violence in marriage, Maggie went on to a second practical step. The second step was this: respond to your mate with tangible kindness. This meant that Maggie was to do some concrete good to Fred.

Maggie and I talked at some length about what that might mean. We came up with a number of things that Fred would call "good." Among these were (1) a regular systematic reading of the food-sale papers (2) faithful use of free coupons (3) acceptance of, and compliance with, Fred's limit on the food budget, and (4) new efforts to be creative in the kitchen, paying particular attention to Fred's favorite dishes.

Finally, the third step in introducing non-violence into the marriage: forgiveness. Forgive Fred from the heart. Whatever faults he had, whatever sins he had committed, Fred was to be given a full pardon so that Maggie would be obedient to the command of her Lord.

These were all concrete efforts to carry forth a program of love in a very violent marriage. True, it was a very difficult program, but the alternative was marital warfare. It was understandable that Maggie suggested "new" ways to be non-violent. Her idea was simply to be quiet, to give Fred the silent treatment in their disputes. That is non-violent but there is no love in it. The true peacemaker must love intentionally, first by means of verbal self-criticism, then by seeking to do positive good to the "enemy," and finally, by means of genuine forgiveness.

POWER GREATER THAN OURSELVES

Non-violence is a technique, a method, a strategy based on love. The best place to make a beginning with non-violence in this hate-filled world is in marriage. There the need is the greatest because there is no pain to compare with marital warfare. Place all forms of pain on the table and marital pain will tower above them all.

The need for a non-violent solution in marriage is the more urgent because children, the fruit of marriage, need to be raised on the basis of non-violent principles. The radical principle of non-violent love must be instilled early in the human heart. From there, it needs to find expression in society, government, and, not least, the church, which at times can be so loveless.

There is power in love—*God's* power.

10

Power in the Church

Among the last promises of our Lord to His church, was the assurance that "you shall receive power when the Holy Spirit has come upon you" (Acts 1:8). And never was power so sorely needed. The infant church had been entrusted with an astonishing message from another world. The message was this: all egocentrics who surrender to the Highest Power will live eternally. But those who willfully insist on being the highest power in their own lives are lost. This radical message was from Jesus Christ, the Son of God, himself the Highest Power. A blanket forgiveness was promised to everyone who obeyed this message.

From what we can gather from the biblical record, the disciples were selected by Jesus himself as the persons vested with power to rule the infant church. Peter, however, seems to have been given some pre-eminence. There is no escaping from the obvious meaning of our Lord's words to Peter: "And I tell you, you are Peter, and on this rock I will build my church, and the powers of death shall not prevail against it. I will give you the keys of the kingdom of heaven, and whatever you bind on earth shall be bound in heaven, and whatever you loose on earth shall be loosed in heaven" (Matt. 16:18-19).

There was a very good reason why our Lord gave Peter (and later, the other disciples) the keys of the kingdom. It is because power is nothing until it is vested in persons.

That statement needs some explanation.

POWER GREATER THAN OURSELVES

Power is always personal. Our Lord understood that it would be useless to bestow power to rule upon the entire body of believers. Jesus, in the instance of Matthew 16, selected eleven who were given responsibility to rule (to bind and loose) with Peter given an explicit charge. Paul did the same thing in the churches he established. He ordained elders whom he kept under his direct control through written epistles. None of the epistles were intended as friendly advice. They were orders from the apostles, given in a context of love.

Once again, power is always a personal thing. If you bestow power indiscriminately on a group, the group will simply produce a leader who will take power and use it on others. Every group invariably produces its own leader. The emergent leader takes power and uses it on his followers, most of whom are usually quite passive. A few of them, though, will wait for an opportunity to rebel.

In the first century, the Church at Rome seemed immediately to have emerged as the leading church. Twenty-five years after Pentecost, Paul wrote his Epistle to the Romans. By then (A.D. 56), the Church of Rome was an active, thriving assembly of believers. Both Peter and Paul are believed to have died as martyrs in Rome. The spiritual vitality of the church, the presence of Peter, the mystique of the Eternal City all established the Roman Church as the dominant power in first century Christianity.

The Church at Rome continued to exert leadership in spite of a challenge from Constantinople in the fourth century. After that, the leadership and power in the Christian Church rested in the hands of the Roman Catholic Church, though there were serious challenges from thirty-seven antipopes and the defection of Eastern Orthodoxy in A.D. 1054. One man, the pope, held both the highest power and the authority to use it. The pope was surrounded by the College of Cardinals and a host of experts which would serve with him advice. But final decisions were left in the hands of one man—the pope.

The Reformers—Luther, Calvin, Zwingli—who disagreed among themselves on so many matters, were united in this: no longer would they recognize the authority of the Roman pontiff over them. The Reformers broke with Roman Catholicism and established their separate Protestant churches. The Lutherans, the Calvinists, and the Anabaptists all organized themselves in such a way that binding decisions were reached only by delegated representatives sent by the local congregations to higher church bodies. No more of that one-man rule as in Catholicism. Now delegates would *vote* on what to believe and what to do as a church. Anyone who could not accept such a church polity and the decisions of these representative assemblies was excommunicated.

It is now almost five hundred years since the Reformation began. That is a sufficient lapse of time to see how Protestants have used the power of the keys of the kingdom. For sure, we are confronted today with some extremely diflficult problems with regard to the use of the power assumed around 1517. I wish to list three problems peculiar to Protestant church polity.

1. What we have discovered, to our embarrassment, is that the majority in any church assembly, does not always vote for the truth. This is something, it seems, on which the Reformers had not counted. Their zeal was so great in disposing of the pope that they did not foresee the problem of determining what was right and true by asking church assemblies to vote on it. Let me give one example of this.

There is today in all Protestant churches one bloc of voting delegates who are conservative and another who are the liberals. I understand even the Unitarians have conservative blocs in them and, of course, every conservative denomination has its liberal wing. Now, when an issue regarding credal beliefs or church polity is brought before a church's highest assembly, the matter is thoroughly discussed and then brought to a vote by the assembly. That vote, we now know, is basically mindless. That is the word to use— mindless—because the final decision is determined on the basis of a majority vote rather than by a rational decision made on the basis of facts and principles. A single trusted person has the advantage of at least being able to separate truth from error. Conservative blocs in opposition to liberal blocs cannot do that. The outcome of the vote has nothing to do with what is right or wrong, true or false. The final decision is determined by which side has the most power in the form of a majority of the votes.

There is no doubt but that representative assemblies are the best way to govern nations. In such nations, the majority rules. The minority may quarrel about the decision, but normally, an issue is settled with a vote of the elected representatives. The purpose of the vote is to settle important issues and get on with living according to the will of the majority. The point to observe here, however, is that a nation does not presume to define God's eternal truth and will. Churches do—or, at least, should.

2. A second problem peculiar to Protestant church polity is that, having rid ourselves of the Roman pontiff, new Protestant popes keep on springing up. This began with those strong personalities, Martin Luther and John Calvin. When they spoke, it was usually accepted as the final word.

I recall as a boy in the Christian Reformed Church the authority and prestige of Professor Louis Berkhof, professor of dogmatic theology at Calvin Seminary. Professor Berkhof looked like an Old Testament patriarch. He was very tall, a big man with a distinguished head of gray hair.

My father, who was greatly interested in church affairs, always studied the ideas of Berkhof on any important issue. If Berkhof said something was true, that was enough for father! Indeed, Professor Berkhof had tremendous prestige at the yearly meeting of synod. His ideas and opinions were sought out. He was widely quoted. When the votes were counted on the important issues, they usually came out close to the positions of the denomination's unofficial leader, Professor Berkhof.

Not all Protestant power-people are visible. Many work in the background, away from public scrutiny. As I look around at various denominations, however, I observe a few power brokers near the top of each denomination. Out of that elite group there usually emerges one person who wields most power. He is, unofficially, a pope.

It is almost predictable, now that we think about it, that Protestant denominations would each produce their own leader. This is understandable if we truly understand that power is *always* personal. Committees, for example, do not have power. They begin to get power when one individual picks up the power conferred on the committee and leads with it, the others following. Such a leader can conceivably collect power far beyond what was officially given him—and get away with using it.

Just as committees have no power until one person picks it up, so denominations are basically run by people who have either taken or been given power. Synodical decisions do form a considerable restraint upon the unbridled use of power by a power-person. But where there is no place for the exercise of power, the talented power-people will create such a place.

3. In the struggle between Pope Leo X and Martin Luther, we can see what the Reformation was really about. The Reformation, at least initially, was a classic power-struggle between two very powerful men. Their basic point of dispute had to do with the nature of authority—that is, how power is to be used.

Pope Leo X insisted upon submission to papal authority. Luther rejected papal authority, substituting in its place the believer's direct submission to scriptural authority, basing that on the priesthood of all believers. This left Luther with a problem which is still unsolved among Protestants. If you tell a believer to interpret the Scriptures according to his own understanding, it is a little like asking a U.S. citizen to apply the principles of the U.S. Constitution without using the court system to make binding decisions to individual cases.

The various denominations have, therefore, written their creeds and established their ecclesiastical courts in order to control the interpretation of Scripture. Anyone who is unhappy with his present church, however, can either join another church or begin a new one. This is what faithfulness to the Scriptures means to the Protestant mind.

All this has caused some of us Protestants to wonder whether we have not built a monument to our rebellion, rather than establishing the true church.

TWELVE SUGGESTED STEPS
OF ALCOHOLICS ANONYMOUS

1   We admitted we were powerless over alcohol—that our lives had become unmanageable.
2   Came to believe that a Power greater than ourselves could restore us to sanity.
3   Made a decision to turn our will and our lives over to the care of God *as we understood Him.*
4   Made a searching and fearless moral inventory of ourselves.
5   Admitted to God, to ourselves and to another human being the exact nature of our wrongs.
6   Were entirely ready to have God remove all these defects of character.
7   Humbly asked Him to remove our shortcomings.
8   Made a list of all persons we had harmed, and became willing to make amends to them all.
9   Made direct amends to such people wherever possible, except when to do so would injure them or others.
10 Continued to take personal inventory and when we were wrong promptly admitted it.
11 Sought through prayer and meditation to improve our conscious contact with God *as we understood Him,* praying only for knowledge of His will for us and the power to carry that out.
12 Having had a spiritual awakening as the result of these steps, we tried to carry this message to alcoholics, and to practice these principles in all our affairs.

11

Power and Alcoholics Anonymous

A miracle is happening right before our eyes. Most of the world does not know about it. It is possible to look squarely into the face of a miracle and not recognize it. But the miracle is *there*. And it is of God. This miracle is called Alcoholics Anonymous.

This large company of people—one million in thirty-two thousand groups—now belong to AA. They have been given nothing less than the solution to the problem of power. As individuals they have made peace with Higher Power. As a group, they have learned how to effectively govern themselves through Alcoholics Anonymous. AA is one of the most incredible stories of the twentieth century. It offers all kinds of constructive suggestions to us who are students of the phenomenon of power.

Look first with me at one alcoholic individual in his drinking days. This person is composed of pure ego. That is, *he* is his own highest power. With god-like omnipotence, he declares that he has sufficient power to handle any problems he might encounter, including his so-called drinking problem. Indeed, who else will solve this problem if not he? So far as this so-called alcohol problem is concerned, others control their drinking and even quit altogether when they wish. Why can he not do the same? His greatest present problem, he declares, is an unfair distrust, a failure to understand, a lack of support on the part of those close to him. His despairing word to us is this: "Leave me alone. I have everything under control!" He may never change. The wise counsel of friends may always be interpreted as an attack upon him. He is unyielding in his delusion that he is supremely right in his judgments and sufficiently powerful to solve all his problems.

Thousands die in such delusions.

The tragedy of such a death is that the problem of egocentricity is left totally unresolved. Such a person leaves the world as much an egocentric as when he entered it. No transformation. No growth. Only eternal tragedy. What could have been, will never be.

By the grace of God, an increasing number of alcoholic people are escaping this eternal tragedy through the program of Alcoholics Anonymous. This program is spelled out in twelve steps.* Let us look briefly at each step. As you read them, remember that their purpose is to simply offer concrete steps for the human ego to submit (and remain submitted) to the God of all power.

> 1. We admitted we were powerless over alcohol—
>   that our lives had become unmanageable.

First, the *truth*.

The alcoholic is asked to admit the truth that alcohol has complete control over him. He is powerless. Alcohol is completely in charge. And his life is completely out of control!

Before we go one step further with these steps, I want to confess that I, who am not an alcoholic, am fully as egocentric as any practicing alcoholic. My life, moreover, was fully as unmanageable and problematic. I find that what I read in these twelve steps applies just as fully to me as to any alcoholic.

I invite you, my reader, to join us in a declaration of powerlessness over problems and the complete unmanageability of our lives! Our situation is desperate. We are out of control and we have no power to bring things back under our control.

This first step is absolutely crushing to our egos. We had hoped for some help in building our egos. We needed strengthening. We sought

---

* Quotations are used by permission. They are quoted from the book, *Twelve Steps and Twelve Traditions*, Alcoholics Anonymous World Services, Inc.

Power and Alcoholics Anonymous

new power. But this first step slays our egos! We feel powerless.

2. Came to believe that a Power greater than ourselves could restore us to sanity.

You notice how discreetly this step avoids the use of the divine name. God is called a "Power greater than ourselves." Egocentrics, you see, always bristle when any reference is made to Deity. Human gods are very jealous gods. They will tolerate no competition. All deities save one (the egocentric) are false gods. In order not to cause needless offense, therefore, the divine name is not yet mentioned.

The alcoholic person is asked to believe, however, that there is a Power greater than himself. This is the most radical suggestion that can be made to a person who, heretofore, has been the highest power in his world. Obviously, there cannot be two highest powers. Someone must step down. The second step suggests that the alcoholic, rather than God, take this step. A reward is promised him. The alcoholic will have his sanity restored to him.

Notice, however, that at the point of this second step, there is a terrible storm still raging in the alcoholic's heart. The reason for the tempest is simply that the conflict between Higher Power and the alcoholic's ego-power has not yet been resolved.

There is, however, a new element in the struggle. It is *hope*. The alcoholic has been given reason to believe that all is not lost. There is hope, a hope which promises relief from his loneliness, his intense suffering and his insane behavior.

And so a tiny place has been made in the alcoholic's world for a Power whose glory fills heaven and earth. It is God's achievement, not a human achievement. But for the grace of God, all egocentrics would continue to endlessly orbit around the Self.

3. Made a decision to turn our will and our lives over to the care of God as we understand Him.

This is the key step in the AA program. The first two steps build up to it. The last nine steps flow from it.

Step three is a call to action, the act of surrendering one's will and life to God.

POWER GREATER THAN OURSELVES

Notice how this action ignores any mental objections we might have to this step. Our sponsor does not give a lengthy explanation of what we are to do. Nor does he tell us why we are surrendering. He just asks us to do it.

We note, also, that in the act of surrendering, our emotions are ignored. We are given a full freedom to feel as we wish. No one is asked to enjoy self-surrender. A person is merely asked to turn over his will and his life to the care of God as he understands Him.

The issue in this third step is once again power—"I-will-power." We are asked to make a clear, definite decision between human power and Divine Power. A sweet, sentimental religion teaches us that we can have both powers working in tandem. A Christ-less intellectual religion tells us that, if we are unhappy with the idea, we do not even need God. But a religion with the Living God and a perishing god-player must involve insistence on the necessity of a complete capitulation to Divine Power.

"Instead of using 'our will power,' as everyone outside of AA seems to think we do, we give up our wills to a Higher Power, place our lives in hands—invisible hands—stronger than ours." (*Alcoholics Anonymous,* p. 340)

AA people express the miracle in various ways. One says, "We surrender to win." Another says, "We give away to keep." Still another says, "We suffer to get well." One more says, "We die to live" (p. 341-2).

They each say it well. They all say the same thing.

4. Made a searching and fearless moral inventory of ourselves.
5. Admitted to God, to ourselves, and to another human being, the exact nature of our wrongs.
6. Were entirely ready to have God remove all these defects of character.
7. Humbly asked Him to remove our shortcomings.
8. Made a list of all persons we had harmed, and became willing to make amends to them all.
9. Made direct amends to such people wherever

possible, except when to do so would injure them or others.
10. Continued to take personal inventory and when we were wrong promptly admitted it.

Steps four through ten speak of a personal moral inventory. It is unnecessary to comment on each step, but I do wish to reflect briefly on these seven steps as a group.

Why all this searching within ourselves? Why persist in this moral inventory? Why the constant introspection?

Simply to demolish ego-power.

We are encouraged to speak the unspeakable about ourselves. To insure our honesty and humility, we invite another person to hear the awful truth about our lives. We next go to God, asking Him to forgive and heal us. Then we must make amends to the people we have hurt. All this slays us. We agree, finally, to continue moral inventory as a regular habit.

We hate it, but we do it.

If we do not do it, we will perish.

All power has gone out of us. We are weak.

Finally, God has the power.

11. Sought through prayer and meditation to improve our conscious contact with God as we understood Him, praying only for knowledge of His will for us and the power to carry that out.
12. Having had a spiritual awakening as the result of these steps, we tried to carry this message to alcoholics, and to practice these principles in all our affairs.

Recovering alcoholics with considerable experience in AA tell me that twelve step work is often difficult and dirty. It is difficult because practicing alcoholics who have hit the bottom often bounce at the bottom of the world for an amazing period of time. Very little can be done until the person realizes he needs help. Meanwhile, he will use his considerable bag of tricks to continue drinking. All of this works against successful completion of the twelve steps.

Such work is also dirty—literally. Those who suffer from severe alcoholism often lose control of their bodily functions. Add to this an arrogant willful mind which will not take advice.

Working with such people, however, does have a redeeming benefit. It keeps the twelve stepper humble. And sober.

Less familiar than the twelve steps are the twelve traditions of Alcoholics Anonymous. As the twelve steps solve the problem of power for the individual, so the twelve traditions solve the problem of power for the group. Indeed, AA aims at the submission of human power to Divine Power as much in its group life as in individuals.

Below are the twelve traditions. Following them, I wish to make four comments.

1. Our common welfare should come first; personal recovery depends upon AA unity.
2. For our group purpose there is but one ultimate authority—a loving God as He may express himself in our group conscience. Our leaders are but trusted servants; they do not govern.
3. The only requirement for AA membership is a desire to stop drinking.
4. Each group should be autonomous except in matters affecting other groups or AA as a whole.
5. Each group has but one primary purpose—to carry its message to the alcoholic who still suffers.
6. An AA group ought never endorse, finance or lend the AA name to any related facility or outside enterprise, lest problems of money, property and prestige divert us from our primary purpose.
7. Every AA group ought to be fully self-supporting, declining outside contributions.
8. Alcoholics Anonymous should remain forever

non-professional, but our service centers may employ special workers.

9. AA, as such, ought never be organized; but we may create service boards or committees directly responsible to those they serve.

10. Alcoholics Anonymous has no opinion on outside issues; hence the AA name ought never be drawn into public controversy.

11. Our public relations policy is based on attraction rather than promotion; we need always maintain personal anonymity at the level of press, radio and films.

12. Anonymity is the spiritual foundation of our traditions, ever reminding us to place principles before personalities.

1. Alcoholics Anonymous, supposedly composed of power-mad individuals with massive egos, *has never had a schism since its founding in 1935.* It seems more than likely that the unity of AA will never be broken.

As I search AA literature and study their groups, the only reason I can find for this miraculous unity is that they *never* use power on their people. The twelve traditions do not contain a single "don't." They never say "You must." Nor are there conditions for membership, except for a desire to stop drinking. A person is a member of AA when *he* says he is a member.

Superficially, AA looks loosely organized and poorly disciplined. In actual fact, AA has a strength of purpose and action which is irresistible. I know of no comparable twentieth century organization whose use of power is at once so effective and inoffensive.

2. "There is but one ultimate authority—a loving God as He may express himself in our group conscience."

There. The problem of authority and power is settled right there.

God alone is the authority. He will work through the group conscience. No human authority is necessary!

Is that *really* the way it works in AA?

POWER GREATER THAN OURSELVES

I have been working with these people for twenty-five years and I bring this report: it is true. AA has no authority other than God. They are, moreover, among the most happy and productive people I know.

3. AA has defined the term "leader" in almost the exact way that Jesus defined the word.

Our Lord said, "He who is greatest among you shall be your servant; whoever exalts himself will be humbled and whoever humbles himself will be exalted" (Matt. 23:11-12). When Jesus humbly washed His disciples' feet He enacted this principle. "If I then, your Lord and Teacher, have washed your feet, you also ought to wash one another's feet" (John 13:14).

In AA, a leader serves the group by being a good example, by making helpful suggestions and by doing what tasks a group asks him to do. He is a servant, not a ruler. AA has no experts, no professionals.

4. In AA power is used in a unique way. AA groups have power, but they do not use it coercively. The power of an AA group is formidable. A group decision is sufficiently powerful to crush any dissidence, but the defeated are not humiliated, nor are they coerced in any way. There simply are no creeds which must be accepted. There are no punishments to be meted out.

The same principle applies to money. AA is committed to the principle of corporate poverty. There are no dues. Free-will offerings are received as needed and a donor is asked to limit his donations to two hundred dollars per year. Legacies are politely returned. There is no professional staff to support. AA headquarters hires a few special workers to do the necessary office work, but that is all.

Power in AA is channeled only to carrying the AA message to other alcoholics who are drawn by attraction rather than promotion. The purpose of the AA group is limited to this one task. Consistent with this position, AA declines to endorse or support outside causes.

5. An unenforced anonymity at the public level is marvelously effective in helping AA members resist the temptation to make a name for themselves. Members are known simply by their first names. All notoriety is discouraged. Active participation in the work of AA is encouraged.

Power and Alcoholics Anonymous

Most of the current literature on alcoholism asserts that people drink in order to resolve deep dependency needs which were established early in childhood. Such a view sees the child as small, helpless, invariably the victim of poor parenting. The alcoholics with whom I talk in AA usually greet this view with a patient smile and then give *their* reason for drinking.

AA people almost invariably will tell you that they drank because the booze gave them a *sense of power*. True, it was short-lived, but while it lasted, it certainly seemed worth the trouble—at least until the addiction became a dictatorial tyrant. After that, there was a growing sense of powerlessness.

All this makes the recovering alcoholics of AA among the world's greatest authorities on the subject of power. There are four reasons for this:

1. AA people have correctly assessed the strength of willpower. It is pitifully weak. Human strength is impotent in the face of the chemical reaction alcohol produces in the human body. Willpower is strong only in the sense that it willfully, stupidly resists facing the truth.
2. It is Higher Power who saves the surrendered alcoholic from death. This is his message to the world.
3. It is the Higher Power who now keeps the surrendered alcoholic sober a day at a time.
4. These recovering alcoholics, have, by the grace of God, formed themselves into an amazingly effective group which, happily, declines to use power on its members.

12

Power in the Bible

There is no richer treasure on the subject of power than in the Bible. Interestingly, what the Bible has to say about power is not contained in discourses or sermons. Rather, the issue of power is helpfully illustrated in the lives of real, historical people. Best of all, we are given God's solution to the problem of power. It is one of His best gifts to us.

In this chapter I will limit myself to the lives of ten selected people in Bible history. The next chapter will deal with the unique Key to the solution of the problem of power, Jesus Christ.

Adam and Eve

Adam was tempted by the possibility of becoming "like God" (Gen. 3:5). God had forbidden eating from a certain tree in the Garden of Eden. The command of God stood as a challenge to the power of Adam. Here in the first member of the human race, we see how a restrictive command immediately excited man to willfully insist on an insane contest of power. This mad need to contest God's power and authority was not something which through the centuries slowly evolved in human consciousness. It was *there,* as the central issue in human life, from the very beginning.

The Fall of Adam shows us that man cannot set his own limits. He was not intended to do so. Human beings cannot be their own authorities. People were never intended to set the limits of their own power. It is God's prerogative. God is the source of law, not man.

POWER GREATER THAN OURSELVES

The temptation in the Garden of Eden was the first lesson God wanted to teach the human race. It is the lesson of sin. Sin is rebellion against God. Sin is a mad contest of human power against divine power.

Later, God would teach an even greater lesson, the lesson of grace and forgiveness. This means that our arrogant assaults upon God's power and authority need not result in our endless destruction. We can be saved. The possibility of new obedience is open to us. In all transactions with God, we are powerless and obedient. He is the one with the power.

Abraham

It is not surprising that Abraham is given such a high place of honor in the Scriptures. Abraham was a "friend of God" (James 2:23). Because of that relationship, Abraham's life was almost completely free of any struggle against God's power.

Abraham was an obedient man. When God called him out of the Ur of Chaldees, Abraham responded by leaving his home and traveling north. He did not know his destination but trusted God to guide him. Later, in a dispute with Lot of over pasturage, Abraham did not press for his rights. When God commanded Abraham to exile his son Ishmael into the desert, Abraham was obedient. Even when God commanded him to sacrifice Isaac, his son and heir, Abraham did not rebel. Abraham never used power on God—except in one instance.

The decision to fulfill God's promise of an heir through Hagar rather than Sarah (who was very aged and apparently barren) is a clear instance of rebellion against God. The fact that it was well intentioned and what we might call passive rebellion, makes no difference. Abraham's undeniable weakness was the use of power in a passive way.

Abraham is one of the best models of powerlessless in the presence of God. Yet Abraham, a man who sought no power, was given much power. He was extremely rich. It was even possible for him to form a small army capable of crushing a powerful alliance of neighboring tribes. The power of wealth and tribal leadership, however, seems never to have gone to his head. Throughout his life he was humbly obedient to the authority and power of God, which is to say that he was powerless in God's presence.

The lesson of Abraham's life is quite clear and surely very radical: human power is to be shunned, avoided. The accomplishment of God's purpose in our lives is for His power to accomplish. Power is not in man. Later, we shall see this in David, who put it into these words, "Once God has spoken; twice have I heard this: that power belongs to God" (Ps. 62:11).

Joseph

Joseph is a puzzle.

Ten chapters (37-47) of Genesis are devoted to this man who seemed oddly obsessed with power. We know very little about his spirituality. He is difficult to understand, hard to explain.

Consider these odd bits of information given in the Book of Genesis:

1. Joseph evidently relished his position as Father Jacob's favorite son. Jacob gave Joseph the long robe with sleeves as tangible proof of that close relationship. It was unfortunate that Jacob played favorites with Joseph. We can infer that Joseph did nothing to conceal the fact from his brothers. His brothers, understandably, became jealous.

2. Joseph foolishly provoked his brothers' wrath. What placed him in opposition to them was the revelation of two dreams. In the first dream Joseph's wheat-sheaf stood erect while the family's sheaves bowed down to it. In the second dream, the sun, moon and stars bowed down to Joseph. This signified that the family would someday bow down to Joseph.

Joseph was incredibly foolish to reveal his private dreams to his family. By so doing, he kindled even more the wrath of his ten very strong brothers. Their explosive reaction came when Joseph naively walked into their camp at Shechem to investigate their work so as to report to Father Jacob. Only the pleadings of Brother Reuben restrained the brothers from killing him.

So far, we get a picture of Joseph as a very egotistical young man whose special gift seems to have been taunting his brothers. It was not a good sign.

3. Joseph was sold as a slave to Potiphar in Egypt. There Potiphar's wife attempted to seduce him. Joseph was unquestionably virtuous and God-fearing in resisting her advances, but he also had his own interests in mind. It was impossible to gain power in Potiphar's house by yielding to his wife. Potiphar, however, believed his wife when she accused Joseph of attempting to seduce her. He sent Joseph to prison. There he immediately ingratiated himself to the keeper of the prison by his trustworthiness and diligence.

4. In prison, Joseph became known for his ability to interpret dreams. Pharaoh heard of Joseph and, upon having his dream interpreted, received counsel to store up grain against the coming years of famine. Joseph suggested that a man "discreet and wise" be appointed to oversee the grain storage program. Pharaoh promptly appointed Joseph to that position, second only to Pharaoh himself!

I am sure that Joseph got to be second under Pharaoh on the basis of divine providence and some solid ability. But Joseph was also a climber. As with most "wunderkinder" he liked power, knew how to acquire it and later use it.

Joseph's swift rise to power was not brought about solely by his own efforts. Circumstances and divine providence raised him to that position. The test of Joseph's character would come later, when his brothers were forced to travel from their famine-stricken land and beg him for food.

5. Pharaoh gave Joseph complete power over the sale of the precious grain, but Joseph himself trusted no one. He would not delegate the direct sale of the grain to anyone. Joseph himself, evidently, handled each sale. He held onto *all* the power available. This is how he met his brothers.

Joseph greeted his brothers with anger ("he spoke roughly to them") and false accusation ("You are spies"). They were, moreover, locked up in jail until one could fetch Benjamin from Canaan. After three days, the angry Joseph had second thoughts. He decided that one of the brothers must remain in jail while the others returned home to bring Benjamin with them on the next trip.

Joseph, wanting no part of business with his brothers, had their money placed in each sack of grain.

Joseph was clearly dangling his brothers. But why? Some commentators believe that Joseph was attempting to reform his brothers' characters. Possibly, but it seems to me more likely that Joseph simply wanted power over his brothers. He wanted them to obey him.

6. The brothers returned to Joseph a second time for food. They dined with Joseph, still not suspecting who he actually was. The brothers were sent home. But Joseph had commanded that his silver cup be hidden in Benjamin's sack of grain. Joseph's agents overtook the brothers and they were accused of theft. The silver cup was found and they were forced to return.

Again we ask, why all this business of the cat playing with the mouse? Was it for the brothers' sake? Strange. That could have been done far more simply. Was Joseph, the man absorbed with power, retaliating? It appears so.

7. Finally, things came to a climax. Judah heroically offered himself for slavery in Egypt in substitution for Benjamin. It was this demonstration of selflessness and courage which finally moved Joseph away from his obsession with power over his brothers. Joseph broke down, wept, revealed his true identity, and reunited with his brothers.

8. A touching reunion followed. Joseph and Pharaoh both invited his brothers and Father Jacob to live in Goshen. On leaving Egypt with this good news, the brothers were evidently still under some suspicion for they were reminded, "Do not quarrel on the way."

9. The years of famine were very severe in Egypt. The Egyptians came to Joseph to buy food. When the money ran out, they sold their farms to Pharaoh and, finally, themselves into slavery. The commercial policies of Joseph were without any mercy or compassion. Joseph, having his hands on some power, wanted all power under Pharaoh in Egypt.

10. When Jacob died, the brothers still feared retaliation from Joseph. To his credit, this last exchange between the brothers and Joseph shows in him a new level of maturity. Joseph assured them

that there was no need to worry. He would not use power on them as they had feared. It is quite possible that, at the time of Joseph's full maturity, he finally gave up that quest for power which absorbed him throughout his troubled life.

Moses

We are told that Moses was the meekest man in the entire earth (Numbers 12:3). This is an ancient way of saying that Moses sought no power, nor did he use power upon the nation. Moses not only gave us the Law, he lived it. His life history is a consistent record of obedience with only one recorded exception. That was at Meribah.

At Meribah, the nation was without water. Moses was commanded to speak to the rock from which water was to come. Moses chose to do it *his* way. He smote the rock twice with his rod. Water came forth, but also a penalty from the Lord, for this was an attempt to use power against God. The miracle was done Moses' way, not God's. Moses was severely punished by being excluded from Canaan, the Promised Land (Numbers 20:10-13).

Previously, at Mount Sinai, God had used Moses as the Law-giver. The Law revealed to Moses consisted of the moral law (the Ten Commandments), the intricate ceremonial laws of worship and the unbending civil laws under which the people were to worship God. Why all these laws? To teach God's people that power belongs only to the Lord, and that power is not in us. Man is never to use power against the Lord, nor against his fellow-man.

Even a hasty look at the Ten Commandments immediately reveals to us their message about power.

"You shall have no other gods before me." God will not tolerate manufactured deities who oppose Him, the true God. He alone is the Power with whom man is to deal.

"You shall not make for yourself a graven image." Why do people manufacture idols? To get power. Why does a primitive tribesman still today bury a stone image of a fruit at the base of his fruit tree? To get power unto a good harvest.

"You shall not take the name of the Lord your God in vain." Why would anyone want to profane the Divine Name? Only to gain power.

The mental deception behind profanity is well known. One who dares to trample upon the Divine Name does so to experience a sense of power of God Himself.

"Remember the sabbath day, to keep it holy." Human power depletes itself. It is a limited power and needs renewal. The Lord, who needs no rest, yet set us an example, by resting on the seventh day of creation.

"Honor your father and your mother." Parents are God-ordained powers set over us. In childhood, parents are to be obeyed; in adulthood, honored. God abhors any contest of power with them. The child must capitulate.

"You shall not kill."

"You shall not commit adultery."

"You shall not steal."

"You shall not bear false witness against your neighbor."

"You shall not covet . . . ."

Our Lord summarized these Commandments by saying, "You shall love your neighbor as yourself" (Matt. 22:39). The only power we are given with our neighbor is the power to love. Love forbids any domination of another person. Living *with* people *under* God reduces us to a powerlessness which, paradoxically, blesses us with Almighty Power!

Gideon

Gideon lived in a chaotic period of the history of Israel (circa 1125 B.C.). "The hand of Midian prevailed over Israel" (Judges 6:2). Gideon was a nobody, born into a weak clan and of a very poor family.

But God called reluctant, protesting Gideon to leadership and victory, but not through human power. When thirty-two thousand men of Israel responded to a call to arms, ten thousand of them were sent home. When twenty-two thousand men were preparing for battle, God instructed Gideon to send them all to their homes, save three hundred. With this tiny force, Gideon surrounded the Midianite camp at night. The only weapons in their hands were torches and trumpets. Suddenly, the torches were raised with a shout and the trumpets blown. Midian panicked and a rout followed.

In this most troubled time of Israel's history—the period of the judges—God worked one of His best demonstrations of power. There was no power in Israel, nor in Gideon. His victory was wholly of God.

One would think that such a demonstration of divine power in the presence of human powerlessness, would forever convince Gideon that power belongs to God alone.

Not so.

Gideon gathered the gold loot taken from the Midianites and cast it into an idol-image. It was erected in his own city where all Israel worshiped it and "played the harlot after it there."

I have often wondered whether the idol-image was a statue of Gideon himself.

Perhaps we can learn from this that the knowledge of God's power and human impotence are the two ideas most abhorrent to the human mind.

David

David seems to have learned the place of power very early in his life. In the contest with Goliath, David shouted, "You come to me with a sword and with a spear and with a javelin; but I come to you in the name of the LORD of hosts, the God of the armies of Israel, whom you have defied. . . . The LORD saves not with sword and spear; for the battle is the LORD'S and he will give you into our hand" (1 Sam 17:45, 47). David correctly sensed the place of power in life. God would have much use for such a man.

As a young man, David was taken into the court of King Saul. Saul became increasingly hostile toward David, making it necessary for him to flee from the royal court. A jealous, demented Saul, consumed by anger, pursued David like a hunter after an animal. Saul is a classic example of how a person vested with power cannot only become corrupted, but demented as well. For Saul was insane.

David could have taken advantage of Saul but he would not. Saul was the Lord's anointed one. None should touch the Lord's anointed. Saul was twice in David's hands and he was urged by his comrades to slay Saul. David refused to use power against him. *God* would have to remove Saul from the throne. Saul, in God's time, was killed in battle by the Philistines.

The reign of King David was an incessant contest of power which David successfully won. The consolidation of the nation of Israel came first, then the subjugation of the surrounding nations. Finally, David had to quell a revolt within his own family. This made David a man of blood, disqualifying him as the builder of the temple.

The Davidic Psalms give us the clearest picture of the inner life of the man David. Even a cursory reading of the Psalms reveals him as a poetic genius. More importantly, David was a man at peace with God. There was no contest of power between them. David wanted to do God's will which, to him, meant keeping the Law. The beauty and goodness of the Law of God was something which fascinated his mind. David also identified himself completely with the righteous judgments of the Lord, a fact which makes the imprecatory Psalms ("Do not I hate them that hate thee, O Lord") more understandable. The consistent posture of David, however, was one of obedience to, and trust in, God. There is only one recorded exception.

The powerful King David was corrupted by his lust for Bathsheba. While her husband Uriah was fighting a war, David committed adultery with her. She conceived. David then sent her husband into a suicide mission with the Philistines. This was calculated sin, both adultery and murder.

Power can corrupt even those who fear God the most. Even God-fearing geniuses seem to have no resistance to such intoxication. This should alert all of us with fewer abilities and lesser commitment to God that we are far more vulnerable than we realize to the corruption of power.

The prophet Nathan was sent of God to expose the king. David was devastated by the exposure and freely confessed his guilt. Psalm 51 records his deepest feelings. In his confession of sin, David reveals his powerlessness in the presence of God the Judge. There is no contesting the verdict nor any offering of excuses. David casts himself powerlessly on the mercy of a just God. The Lord forgives those of a broken and contrite heart.

POWER GREATER THAN OURSELVES

There is one Psalm in particular in which David records with amazingly clear insight his perception of power's place in our lives. I will quote the passage, Psalm 62, and then conclude this chapter with a few comments on this interesting and instructive passage.

For God alone my soul waits in silence;
from him comes my salvation.
He only is my rock and my salvation,
my fortress; I shall not be greatly moved.

How long will you set upon a man
to shatter him, all of you,
like a leaning wall, a tottering fence?
They only plan to thrust him down from his eminence.
They take pleasure in falsehood.
They bless with their mouths,
but inwardly they curse.

For God alone my soul waits in silence,
for my hope is from him.
He only is my rock and my salvation,
my fortress; I shall not be shaken.
On God rests my deliverance and my honor!
my mighty rock, my refuge is God.

Trust in him at all times, O people;
pour out your heart before him;
God is a refuge for us.

Men of low estate are but a breath,
men of high estate are a delusion;
in the balances they go up;
they are together lighter than a breath.
Put no confidence in extortion,
set no vain hopes on robbery;
if riches increase, set not your heart on them.

Power in the Bible

Once God has spoken;
twice have I heard this:
that power belongs to God;
and that to thee, O Lord, belongs steadfast love.
For thus dost requite a man
according to his work.

God is compared to a rock, a fortress and a refuge. These are all terms of power. The power is further defined as a *saving* and *delivering* power, indicating that Divine Power is active to save.

The recipient of divine salvation waits to be saved in quiet confidence ("I shall not be greatly moved.") All human help is useless. God alone can save.

We are urged to trust only in God and turn aside from *all* men, for they are but a breath and a delusion. When weighed they are always found wanting, not to mention guilty. Moreover, riches and wealth—those symbols of human power—are not to be trusted.

David then expresses his deepest understanding of the human condition. He prepares us for his best insight with these words: "Once God has spoken; twice have I heard this . . . ." And then this significant statement: "Power belongs to God."

It has taken me twelve chapters to say what David has said in four words.

Yet I feel I have been a miser with words compared to the volumes of books which today say the opposite of Psalm 62.

As we saw before, in chapter six, the entire world of psychology and psychiatry says that power belongs to man. Behavioral scientists deeply believe in *man*. According to them, God is a poetic name used in a book of fiction called the Bible. The Bible is simply a collection of stories similar to Aesop's *Fables*.

Much of this secular, humanistic philosophy has seeped into religion. There it is presented as "the power of positive thinking" and "the power of possibility thinking." Paul C. Vitz, in his book *Psychology as Religion: the Cult of Self-Worship* (Eerdmans, 1977) points out that "this emphasis on having faith in the self reduces God to a useful servant of the individual in his quest for personal goals" (p. 72).

POWER GREATER THAN OURSELVES

Positive thinking and possibility thinking have no power. Their assumption is that, by a change in our thinking or attitude, divine power will flow into our lives and we will then get what we truly want. We have to get the *right* attitude.

But what *is* the right attitude? Surely not to get something which I really want, as the "thinkers" suggest. The *right* attitude is to have no goals but *God's* goals and to have no power save *God's* power.

Daniel

The contribution of Daniel to our study can be stated quite briefly.

Daniel would testify that under no circumstances or conditions may we ever agree that there is power in humanistic, popular religion.

King Nebuchadnezzar threw Shadrach, Meshach and Abednego into a fiery furnace for refusing to worship a golden image. It makes no difference if the golden image was only a symbol of the nation, or that it represented merely popular religion, that bowing the knee to it was simply an act of patriotism. It is as sinful to worship a nation as an image. Power is in neither one. Power is in God alone.

The Jews were tested a second time when King Darius signed a law stating that, for a period of one month, prayers should be offered to no god nor man save the king. Evidently, all the Jews except Daniel complied with the royal order. Daniel understood very well that the king had the power and authority to destroy him. But the king had no power to change Daniel's conviction that power belongs to God alone.

The Lord did not spare Daniel from being thrown to the lions, but He did deliver him from being devoured by the lions. Divine power alone preserved this God-fearing man.

The lesson for us is clear. In a contest between divine power and human power, divine power will ultimately prevail. Therefore, align yourself with divine power. It is a simple, profound truth which we need to hear in this day when human power seeks to supplant the power of God.

Power in the Bible

Peter

Before Pentecost, Peter was a pathetic example of powerlessness. He was also clumsy and often got in the Lord's way.

The first example of powerlessness was on the Sea of Galilee. Peter dared to walk on the water and succeeded until he looked at another power: the wind on the waves. Peter's faith in divine power vanished. With it vanished the power to transcend nature.

Our Lord's purpose, it seems, was to keep Peter in a posture of powerlessness. He had to stand by helplessly and watch his Lord do the work. In the Garden of Gethsemane, Peter took his sword and cut off a man's ear. Wrong again. Jesus rebuked Peter and healed the wounded man. Later, Peter found himself unable to do anything but deny his Lord when people accused him of being one of Jesus' disciples. Every time Peter opened his mouth, the result was a demonstration of his weakness.

Even after the resurrection, Peter remained powerless. He returned to his old trade—fishing. On one occasion he and his companions had fished all night and caught nothing. Jesus, posing as a solitary beachcomber, told them to fish the opposite side of their boat. Then they lacked the strength to land the large catch, or, for that matter, to do anything right. . . . Until Pentecost.

Pentecost was a great explosion of God's power. And that weak man, Peter, was at the center of it! No sooner had the Holy Spirit fallen upon the believers than Peter emerged as a solid leader who immediately spoke with authority. His pentecostal sermon was powerfully used by the Holy Spirit to gather three-thousand souls into the church. This unorganized body of believers immediately looked to the apostles for guidance. It was Peter, however, who told them what to do: "Repent, and be baptized . . . ."

A new power—the Holy Spirit—had seized Peter and was using him as a channel of divine grace. We next see Peter in the temple, seizing a forty-year-old congenital cripple by the hand, healing him and sending him on his way, "walking and leaping and praising God" (Acts 3:8). This miracle set the stage for Peter's second sermon. Peter's first words clarify the question about the source of power for this miracle. "Men of Israel, why do you wonder at this, or why do you stare at us, as though by our own power or piety we had made him walk? . . . The Faith which is through Jesus has given the man this perfect health . . ." (Acts 3:12, 16). Peter acknowledged the source of his new power. It was the Holy Spirit.

This new Power that possessed Peter was now to make an even greater disclosure. The Power working with Peter could even bring death to those who deceived the Holy Spirit. Ananias and Sapphira, who pretended to share all their property with the believers, gave testimony to this fact by their untimely deaths. Notice that it was not by Peter's command that Ananias lost his life. The Holy Spirit chose that severe penalty, showing that the Power working in Peter was in no way limited by him.

The power of the Holy Spirit continued to work through Peter. Multitudes of believers were added to the church through his ministry. Sick people were healed by the mere touch of his shadow. Tabitha was raised from the dead. Peter was twice miraculously delivered from prison.

Perhaps the greatest demonstration of the power of God in Peter, it seems to me, will always be the Jerusalem Conference. Peter was the acknowledged leader among the brethren. The issue before them was whether Gentile converts should be subject to the Mosaic Law. Peter knew exactly what to say to that crucial question. The Lord had made it clear to Peter in a vision that nothing was unclean to the Christian believer and that Gentiles were full members of the Christian Church.

A beautiful harmony, moreover, existed between Peter and Paul. One looks in vain for evidence of rivalry at the Jerusalem Conference. We could expect that. The issue of power had been decisively settled in the lives of both men. The power was not them. It was God.

Paul

Whereas Peter came to Jesus without any impressive credentials, Paul, before his conversion, was loaded with human power. He was a consummate Jew, the highest product of first century Judaism.

Power in the Bible

Consider who he was. As to status, he was both a Pharisee and a Roman citizen. Both distinctions made him an elite person. He had, moreover, studied under the great Gamaliel during Paul's formative years in Jerusalem. With this excellent training, Paul was not merely a Jew attempting to know and keep the Law. He *knew* it and *kept* it, with enthusiasm. The future looked very good for this extraordinarily bright young Jew. By any human calculation, Paul would go right to the top. He was already distinguishing himself by his ruthless persecution of Christians. Paul had power and he was using it.

But God had other plans for Paul. He would go to the top all right, but Paul, already far up his own mountain, discovered he was on the wrong one! Divine Power confronted him on the road to Damascus. The power was in the form of light. Jesus Christ was a blinding light, a Power that left Paul lying powerless on the Damascus road. It was Paul's first and greatest lesson in God's use of Power.

Paul was led by the hand to Damascus. For three days he lay helpless, blinded and without food or water. Ananias, a very early Christian, brought healing and the gift of the Holy Spirit to Paul. He immediately went to the synagogues of Damascus.

The three missionary journeys of Paul are the record of God's power, through Paul, among people of every nation. Paul, the missionary, was constantly dealing with the issues of power as he traveled the first century world. We can discern three types of power against which he was pitted.

1. *The power of paganism.*

Paul's first missionary tour brought him immediately face to face with paganism. On Cyprus, a magician by the name of Bar-Jesus opposed the gospel Paul was bringing to the proconsul. Paul did not argue or threaten. He simply afflicted the magician with blindness. This was the first of many encounters with paganism. At Lystra an enthusiastic crowd identified the missionaries with Zeus and Hermes. Athens had its altar to an unknown god and Ephesus its temple of Diana. At Philippi the problem was divination. The power of paganism, then, as well as today, was impressive. Paul opposed that power with the power of the Holy Spirit.

111

POWER GREATER THAN OURSELVES

2. *The power of the Jews.*

Paul immediately met the organized resistance of the Jewish power structure. As a missionary, it was Paul's strategy to always go first to the synagogue to preach the gospel. Such a ministry was wonderfully successful with the honest searcher who was looking for the Messiah. The power-people in each synagogue, however, were invariably offended simply because this teaching was not theirs. They had no control over this new teaching. Indeed, they were opposed to it and offended by it. So, for example, we read that at Antioch, "when the Jews saw the multitudes, they were filled with jealousy, and contradicted what was spoken by Paul, and reviled him" (Acts 13:45). This was the pattern throughout Paul's missionary journeys.

Even with the church Jewish power seemed to have exerted a heavy influence. At the Jerusalem Conference, some believers who had formerly been Pharisees contended that Gentile converts had to be circumcised and also keep the Mosaic Law. The Epistle to the Galatians describes well the destructive influence of power-minded Jews who wanted to control the infant church.

3. *The power of Rome.*

Paul was a Roman citizen from birth. He had, therefore, some power which most Jews did not possess. Roman citizens, for example, were exempt from the punishment of crucifixion. As a Roman citizen, Paul was also exempt from scourging with rods and whips. Evidently, Paul was reluctant to use his rights as a Roman citizen because he was beaten three times with rods and five times with whips.

Roman citizens also had the right to be sent to Rome for trial before the emperor himself. Paul could have appealed to Rome a number of times, but, again, he was extremely reluctant to use this right. Why? We can only guess at the reason.

My own opinion is that Paul saw the use of temporal power as a repudiation of spiritual power. Paul had dedicated himself to the demonstration of *spiritual* power, not temporal power. By choosing the path of suffering rather than special privilege, Paul was showing in his own body the submission of his spirit to authority, even in cases where that authority was in error. Paul chose to suffer unjust punishment in order to teach others, and possibly himself also, that his cause was just and his words were truth. His willingness to powerlessly endure suffering was the most effective witness he could make to his Lord. It was Paul's way of being non-violent.

Every student of the Bible knows, however, that Paul *did* appeal to Caesar. Was it the best decision to do so? It is arguable. I am inclined to the view that it was the wrong decision. If Paul had not appealed, he would have been set free by Festus. It was another case of where doing nothing would have been the best decision. God seems to do most when we simply wait. Is it not the Lord's usual way that before He acts, He waits for all lesser power to defer to Him?

> From of old no one has heard
>   or perceived by the ear,
> no eye has seen a God besides thee,
>   who works for those who wait for him.
>   Isaiah 64:4

13

Jesus Christ and Power

> And Jesus came and said to them, "All authority in heaven and on earth has been given to me." (Matt. 28:18)

This is surely one of the most sweeping statements Jesus ever made. Jesus claims here to possess total authority.

What is authority? It is the lawful right to use power.

Authority and power must go together. Authority is useless without power and power is useless without authority. If Jesus had authority to rule, but no power, His authority would have been useless. And power lacking authority is lawless.

Jesus claims *all* authority.

We understand.

This is the voice of God speaking. Only He could say such a thing. But does He have all power as well?

Let us read the Gospels.

> And Jesus returned in the power of the Spirit into Galilee. (Luke 4:14)

Jesus was tempted in the wilderness for forty days.

The devil said, "If you are the Son of God, command this stone to become bread" (Luke 4:3).

Jesus had such power but he declined to use it.

The devil next showed Jesus the kingdoms of the world. "To you

I will give all this authority . . . if you . . . will worship me" (Luke 4:6-7).

Jesus again declined.

Finally, Satan tempted Jesus to throw Himself off the temple, for, according to Scriptures, angels would surely guard him from injury.

Jesus once more refused.

All this was accomplished by the power of the Holy Spirit. Luke tells us Jesus was full of the Holy Spirit. Mark reports that Jesus was driven by the Holy Spirit. Now, as Jesus leaves the wilderness, He "returned in the power of the Spirit into Galilee" (Luke 4:14).

> God anointed Jesus of Nazareth with the Holy Spirit and with power; how he went about doing good and healing all that were oppressed by the devil, for God was with him. (Acts 10:38)

These words are from a sermon by Peter. He was very close to the Lord. Peter knew firsthand the divine power of Jesus.

In this report from Peter, notice his restraint in describing Jesus. Peter resists a lengthy description of Jesus' power.

The Holy Spirit and power are inseparably connected by Peter.

> But that you may know that the Son of man has authority on earth to forgive sins—he said to the paralytic—"I say to you, rise, take up your pallet and go home." (Mark 2:10-11)

The first words of Jesus to the paralytic were, "My son, your sins are forgiven" (2:5). The scribes—those doctors of religious laws—immediately questioned the authority of Jesus to say that, "Who can forgive sins but God alone?" (2:7).

It was a good and fair question.

Jesus answered it by saying that the divine authority to forgive is proven by the divine power to heal. If Jesus had authority and power to heal the man, it meant He also had authority and power to forgive sins.

Indeed, He possesses both and nothing has changed since the day the paralytic was forgiven and healed.

Jesus Christ and Power

> "Teacher, do you not care if we perish?" And he
> awoke and rebuked the wind and said to the sea,
> "Peace! Be still!" And the wind ceased, and there
> was a great calm. (Mark 4:38, 39)

Jesus' power over the stormy sea was as surprising to the disciples as it is to us. It certainly was impressive to see Jesus heal sick people and cast out demons, but stilling a storm at sea struck the disciples as one of the most dramatic demonstrations of Christ's divine power. Yes, only divine power could perform such miracles.

Some of us have come to understand that our Lord even has control over the stormy seas in our minds. There can be a storm in the human mind which seems even more violent and dangerous than an ocean storm. Jesus Christ has the power to still all storms, within us and around us.

> There is a lad here who has five barley loaves and
> two fish; but what are they among so many?
> (John 6:9)

Jesus has divine power to create.

The Gospel of John tells us, "He was in the beginning with God; all things were made through him, and without him was not anything made that was made" (1:2). He who created the world and the universe would surely find it a small thing to feed five thousand from a Galilean boy's lunch. Divine power easily multiplies what is ridiculously inadequate.

> I am the vine, you are the branches. He who abides
> in me, and I in him, he it is that bears much fruit, for
> apart from me you can do nothing. (John 15:5)

Nothing? Lord, are we *that* dependent on Your power?

Our Lord answers again, "Apart from me you can do nothing." That means that our power comes only from His power. Suddenly the subject we are studying—power—becomes very personal. The power we need to live out these lives must flow from our Lord, as surely as sap flows from the trunk of a tree to its branches.

117

POWER GREATER THAN OURSELVES

So we are vastly more dependent upon God in Christ than we realize.

> Thou hast given him power over all flesh, to give
> eternal life to all whom thou hast given him. (John
> 17:21)

This is Jesus, speaking of Himself, in the opening words of the high-priestly prayer. God the Father has given the Son power over all flesh.

Christ's mighty deeds during His three-year ministry certainly proved that He had power over all flesh. The only thing that "limited" his power was unbelief. When Jesus returned a second time to Nazareth where He grew up, we read that "he did not do many mighty works there, because of their unbelief" (Matt. 13:58).

This means that the power of Jesus Christ does not coerce us. We are never crushed, coerced nor cast off. He will:

> . . . feed his flock like a shepherd, He will
> gather the lambs in his arms,
> He will carry them in his bosom,
> And gently lead those that are with young.
> (Isa. 40:11)

> No one takes [my life] from me, but I lay it
> down of my own accord. I have power to
> lay it down, and I have power to take it
> again. (John 10:18)

You and I have power to lay down our lives for a cause. We have no power, however, to prevent our lives from being taken from us. Nor, once our lives are taken from us, can we take them back again. Such power is only Christ's. It is divine power and it is omnipotent.

Therefore, it was unnecessary for Peter, in the Garden of Gethsemane, to reach for the sword to protect Christ. He declined the use of such power, for it was no power at all. Christ already possessed infinite power.

Jesus Christ and Power

"And I, when I am lifted up from the earth, will draw
all men to myself." He said this to show by what
death he was to die. (John 12:32)

Here is another claim which Divine Power makes with complete
self-assurance. He who has set up history will draw to Himself all
nations, all peoples. Jesus Christ does this with His benevolent
power. His executioners knew only destructive malevolent power.
But Christ draws people by an invisible attraction which we call love.

The crucifixion of our Lord was His final statement about power.
Because He was lifted up on a cross, He will draw all men to Him. He
has all power.

But you shall receive power when the Holy Spirit
has come upon you; and you shall be my witnesses
in Jerusalem and in all Judea and Samaria and to
the end of the earth. (Acts 1:8)

This was the final word of our Lord to us. We know that Jesus
always measured and weighed His words carefully. Of all that He
might have said in departing, He chose to say this: "You shall receive
power."

That sure prophecy—fulfilled at Pentecost—answers all our
needs. That power has never been withdrawn from us. Christ's
power is the centerpiece for all of us who have become powerless in
our own strength.

14

The Paradox of Power

This is the word of the Lord . . .
Not by might, nor by power,
but by my Spirit, says the LORD of Hosts.
(Zechariah 4:6)

Ben is a psychologist.

He trained hard for ten years to earn a Ph.D. He always had an honest desire to really help people, and now he was ready.

It took a little while to become established in private practice, but finally he arrived as a professional. He had recognition and prestige.

Three other things, however, were fast catching up with Ben. (1) He no longer believed in secular, self-oriented psychology. It was difficult to admit but he now realized that it was not really helping people. (2) His marriage was collapsing. (3) He was running from God.

At forty, Ben lost most of what had been dear to him. His work and profession were finished. Ben was now in industry. With a great deal of pain, his marriage ended. Everything was gone. Except God.

Ben, that promising, powerhouse of a psychologist, had surrendered his will and his life to God. Ben is powerless in terms of the old power, the false kind of power. Now he knows the power of God is in Jesus Christ.

They that wait for the Lord shall renew their strength,
They shall mount up with wings like eagles,

POWER GREATER THAN OURSELVES

They shall run and not be weary,
They shall walk and not faint.
(Isa. 40:31)

When Anna Young was a young girl of ten, she loved to go riding in the family car each Sunday afternoon. She took with her, of course, an affliction which was always a problem. Anna was severely epileptic.

One Sunday afternoon in 1942, Anna and her parents got into the family car and drove to Skillman, New Jersey. They were to have a picnic lunch there and then return home. The park in which they ate lunch was nicely kept in spite of many large brick buildings nearby.

After lunch, two men dressed in white came to the picnic table. What happened next is still a blur to Anna. Her parents gave her a quick kiss and then the men carried her kicking, scratching and crying into one of the brick buildings. There she was told that this was to be her new home.

The wonder drug, Dilantin, eventually brought Anna's seizures under control but that did not mean she could go home. Her pleas to return home to her parents were rejected. Anna was kept as a ward of the state for a period of forty years. Not only was she detained falsely as a chronic mental patient, but her parents also forbade her to be discharged into the community. An ombudsman from the State of New Jersey urged Anna to sue her parents. She declined.

She declined because the forty year stay in a state institution had developed in her an extraordinary Christian character. She lived very close to God. She waited for the Lord to give her daily strength.

By 1980 her parents were dead and Anna now had opportunity to move into a group home in a nearby community. We all wondered whether, after forty years in a state institution, Anna would be able to function on her own.

We worried in vain. She had long waited on the Lord. She is doing beautifully, enjoying a full life. God has given her abundant strength.

For consider your call, brethren; not many of you were wise according to worldly standards, not many were powerful, not many were of noble birth;

122

The Paradox of Power

but God chose what is foolish in the world to shame the wise, God chose what is weak in the world to shame the strong, God chose what is low and despised in the world, even things that are not, to bring to nothing things that are, so that no human being might boast in the presence of God. He is the source of your life in Christ Jesus, whom God made our wisdom, our righteousness and sanctification and redemption; therefore, it is written, "Let him who boasts, boast of the Lord" (1 Cor. 1:27-28).

It is my privilege to be closely associated with the "low and despised in the world," for such are mental patients in state hospitals.

Toni is a burned-out schizophrenic who is still in a constant struggle with her delusions. She is positive that her right arm is loosely attached to her body and may drop off at any time. When it does, a voice told her that she must have a funeral for it. All her friends will be there throughout the funeral service and they will laugh.

Max is a thirty-eight-year-old retardate. He reads at the second grade level. For the past twenty-five years, Max has lived in a state institution. Many of Max's friends have been discharged into the community, but Max will never leave, though he constantly talks about his home and family.

Bradley is a recovering alcoholic. His liver is severely cirrhotic. According to all the textbooks, Bradley should now be dead. Still, he works and has been accepted back into his family. AA has become a large part of his life. Bradley has learned to live one day at a time, helping other alcoholics.

I count these three people among the three most effective and successful people I know. In a superficial sense they are "nobodies." They have no power, such as we "successful" people count power. They have nothing of which to boast, except God.

God is the source of their "tragic" lives and He has become the source of all good to them. Having nothing in themselves of which to boast, they boast of the Lord—and have everything!

123

POWER GREATER THAN OURSELVES

He said to me, "My grace is sufficient for you, for my power is made perfect in weakness." I will all the more gladly boast of my weaknesses; that the power of Christ may rest upon me. For the sake of Christ, then, I am content with weaknesses, insults, hardships, persecutions, and calamities; for when I am weak, then am I strong. (1 Cor. 12:8)

I visited Alfred in the hospital. He was asleep as I entered. I pulled up a chair and, having some reading material with me, I waited for him to awake.

Alfred: "Are you there, Pastor?"

Earl: "I am, Al, close by."

(silence)

Alfred: "Can you be truthful with me?"

Earl: "I want to be. I think I can."

Alfred: "I am going to die soon. Is that true?"

Earl: "Things do not look good, Al. The diagnosis is cancer."

Alfred: "Oh, God!"

Earl: "Al. Listen to me. This is a time to trust God and let it be."

(pause)

"Let go—Let God."

(pause)

"I want you to fix your mind on God. Have faith in God."

(pause)

"If you are ready to surrender your will and your life into God's hands, take this Bible I have in my hands."

The Paradox of Power

(He slowly reached out for my pocket New Testament.)

"Now repeat after me: 'God's grace is sufficient for me. His power is made perfect in my weakness.' "

In three weeks, Alfred went to his Lord without terror or rebellion. He died as a man of faith, with God as his highest power—and a Bible held tightly in his hands.

15

Conclusions

1. Surrender to God as the Highest Authority is the primary purpose of life. This is why we are here.
2. God's power excludes human power. Human power excludes God's power. The two powers are mutually antagonistic.
3. Human powerlessness is the pre-condition for a display of God's power.
4. Surrender of one's self and life to God must become a way of life if we are to fulfill God's purpose for our lives.
5. The greatest power is love.
6. God is love-power.

16

The Final Word

Once God has spoken,
twice have I heard this:
that power belongs to God;
and that to thee, O Lord,
belongs steadfast love.
(Ps. 62:11)